Conquer Study Stress!

20 Problems Solved

STUDENT-FRIENDLY GUIDES

Conquer Study Stress!
20 Problems Solved

PETER LEVIN

Open University Press

Open University Press
McGraw-Hill Education
McGraw-Hill House
Shoppenhangers Road
Maidenhead
Berkshire
England
SL6 2QL

email: enquiries@openup.co.uk
world wide web: www.openup.co.uk

and Two Penn Plaza, New York, NY 10121-2289, USA

First published 2007

A catalogue record of this book is available from the British Library

ISBN 978 0335 228652

Library of Congress Cataloging-in-Publication Data
CIP data applied for

Typeset by YHT Ltd, London
Printed in the UK by Bell & Bain Ltd, Glasgow

Contents

Preface

Are you a university student and finding studying stressful? If so, the chances are that your teachers think and talk about you as a 'poor' or 'weak' or 'struggling' student. And if the stress that you're experiencing gets you down and you go and see a counsellor, you are likely to find more labels are stuck on you, like 'anxious' and 'depressed'. It's not long before you find yourself brainwashed into seeing yourself as that kind of person.

Is being brainwashed in this way likely to make you a better student, a more effective and efficient learner? I don't expect you think so: I certainly don't.

And the people who stick these labels on you are missing something really important: the ways in which the university environment itself helps to bring about your difficulties, by baffling and confusing you. By the time you've been lectured to in arcane languages, given lists of stuff to read that are so long you haven't a cat in hell's chance of getting through them, and – in particular – tested on your ability to do numerous things you haven't actually been taught to do, arguably the only rational thing to do is to crawl into bed, pull the duvet over your head, and arrange to take up permanent residence there!

The message of this book is that you don't have to take this treatment lying down (so to speak!). You can fight back – and this book shows you how. It deals in turn with 20 common symptoms of stress among students. For each one it first of all highlights the symptom itself, so you can see if it's one that you have got. It then offers a diagnosis, showing how the academic environment – and especially the way in which your institution and people within it treat you – can trigger or help to cause that symptom. It goes on to suggest remedies for the situation: actions that you can take to resist and defeat the environmental causes, and also actions that you can urge your teachers to take. If they co-operate, they can improve matters not only for you but also for your fellow students and future generations of students.

Of course it's very rare for a single cause on its own to give rise to one of these symptoms. Almost always the symptom is the consequence of a number of causes acting as 'contributory factors', combining with one another to bring the symptom about. Some of these factors are environmental but others will be personal: personal to the individual affected. So the same treatment will produce different effects in different people. For example, an unclear instruction, like an ambiguously worded essay topic, could cause one student to retreat in confusion while another regards it as an amusing challenge. This might happen because the former has less self-confidence than the latter, or has a greater propensity to be 'thrown' by unclear instructions.

Perhaps you feel that you don't possess a great deal in the way of self-confidence, or that you are more liable than other students to be 'thrown' by unclear instructions. The good news is that even if your judgement is accurate (and most people are far too hard on themselves), you don't have to stay that way. My experience of listening to students who are under stress, and helping them to work out a way of overcoming it, has taught me this: if you understand what's going on and put the appropriate remedies into effect, you will gain in self-confidence and be able to respond to unclear instructions, mixed messages and other bizarre treatments that universities dish out to students by taking charge of the situation rather than retreating from it in bafflement and confusion. My aim in writing this book is to help you do precisely that.

This book is the seventh in the Student-Friendly Guides series. The others (*Write great essays!, Excellent dissertations!, Sail through exams!, Successful teamwork!, Skilful time management!* and *Perfect presentations!*, co-authored by Graham Topping) all deal with some stressful situations, and so there is inevitably some overlap between this book and those. But you will find that this book complements the others, reinforces their messages, and here and there incorporates further thoughts and responses to comments I have received on the earlier ones.

While the subject of this book is 'stress management', it is very different from other books on that subject. Thus you will find nothing or next to nothing in these pages on diet, exercise, meditation, relaxation or aromatherapy. This book is a 'fight-back' guide to stress management. In that respect it shares 100 per cent the philosophy behind the other Student-Friendly Guides.

Chapter 1

Stressed out by induction

Symptom

I'm a new student and I'm wondering what I've let myself in for. We had a week of welcoming talks, guided tours, incessant queuing and incredibly crowded social events. Now teaching has started I find I'm just one person among hundreds for some lectures and among 20 or more for seminars. I feel quite alienated, in a way.

Diagnosis

You seem to be suffering from a kind of 'culture shock', the shock that you experience when you are removed from a familiar cultural environment and placed in one that feels very new to you. It is a very common phenomenon.

Not only are you in an environment that is new to you – you are among strangers. You probably had to compete to get into university, and now you don't know whether your fellow students are going to be your colleagues or your competitors. You have no idea where your 'place' is: whether there is any kind of 'pecking order' and, if there is, where you come in it. Your previous experience of educational institutions is unlikely to be much help. If you are fortunate you will have a sense of joining a department, but if you are starting on some kind of joint honours degree you may not even have that.

Perhaps too you have a strong sense of being in a minority, of feeling 'marked out' by your gender, your nationality/ethnicity, your religion, the colour of your skin, your sexual orientation, and/or your taste in music and the clothes you wear. If you have come straight from school, or you're a mature student or an international student (especially if English is not your first language), again you may have a feeling of being outnumbered. You may find such feelings very uncomfortable, particularly so if you haven't experienced them before. And among other students there may be cultures – attitudes and ways of behaving – that you find alien and off-putting.

So what does the institution do for you and other new students at this vulnerable initial stage in your university career? It puts you through a process called 'induction'. In the course of this process, the institution gives 'messages' to you. These messages are very likely to be 'mixed': there will be a discrepancy between the message that academics and others think they are giving you and the message that you hear. This discrepancy – these mixed messages – will probably be a main ingredient of the culture shock that you are experiencing.

Institutional cultures in the UK do vary from one institution to another, but there are three features in particular that are commonly found:

- An ethos of elitism
- A prevailing assumption that lectures are an effective way of communicating
- A 'them and us' division between academics and students.

An ethos of elitism. Every head of a university (usually called 'vice-chancellor') and college that provides degree courses, and every head of department, is keen to claim that their outfit is the best at something – or, if not the best, at least in the 'top' few. (Position in 'league tables' is something of an obsession in these circles.) That 'something' could be research, turning out employable graduates, having links with industry, recruiting students from the local community, or 'adding value' to their students.

While the voicing of such claims to new students at induction is understandable – they will want to reassure you that you have come to a place you can be proud of – a note of complacency often creeps in. And this is where mixed messages can arise. The speaker thinks he or she is being friendly and welcoming by congratulating you on joining, especially in the light of the fierce competition for places: you get the message that you should be grateful for being allowed to join. Likewise references to ground-breaking research may be intended to give you a sense of pride, but also convey the message: 'We have more important concerns than teaching.'

A prevailing assumption that lectures are an effective way of communicating. Academics act as though they believe that giving lectures is an effective way of communicating. In practice, as you will soon find out, the lecture is often not an effective medium of communication, and often the audience would learn more by interacting in a different way with their teachers. What does seem to be universally true, however, is that academics do like to have an audience. It gives them a buzz to be up on the dais or platform and, as they think, have dozens of people hanging on their every word. Many of them also transform classes and seminars, which are supposed to be interactive, into lectures, by simply doing all the talking. University managers too like lectures, because they see them as making economical use of staff time: for one teacher to be instructing dozens or hundreds of students at once has to be good value for their money.

During induction, you will not only be subjected to welcome speeches: you will be told, lecture-style, about various services on offer: typically, library, information technology (IT), campus transport; and personal services such as study skills support, counselling, assistance for people with disabilities. The people who address you will think that they are giving you important information and an invitation to make use of the services on offer. You, however, may well be getting different messages: 'We expect you to take in all this information that we're delivering verbally to you' and 'If lots of you ask for personal help, the providers of the service couldn't possibly cope with the demand, so don't feel too warmly invited to take advantage of the service.'

Many universities and other higher education institutions see induction as a suitable time to warn new students about the offence of plagiarism. (Type two the words 'induction' and 'plagiarism' into an Internet search engine and you'll find plenty of instances of this.) The powers that be evidently think that they are giving you important information and a valuable warning. You, however, may get the message: 'We think you are a bunch of potential cheats, and we are watching you closely.'

A 'them and us' division between academics and students. If the welcome you receive in induction is particularly warm, you might get the impression – the message – that you have joined a kind of collective; that you have become a member, albeit a junior one, of a group of people dedicated to learning. Yes, the welcome will be genuine: as new recruits you are a source of money for the institution, and your presence testifies to the institution's or the department's ability to attract applicants; but before long you may pick up hints that collectively you and your fellow students are regarded as a burden ('workload') and as 'the masses' to whom education is to be delivered. In some places, teaching is regarded as a distraction from the important business of research: time spent with students is time lost to research and the production of academic publications.

In short, academics and students have very different interests – and in some important respects their interests conflict.

Remedy

What you should do
If you find yourself having strong emotions, of whatever kind, first of all appreciate that you are in very stress-producing circumstances. Feelings of alienation are common and only to be expected.

Second, make a point of noticing what is going on. Turn yourself into an observer of the academic scene. Ask questions such as:

- Is provision made for students to raise concerns about their studies and any difficulties to do with studying, with personal tutors or other teachers or people with designated pastoral responsibilities?
- Does this institution use IT to facilitate communication between individual students and individual teachers, or primarily to enable teachers to avoid meeting students face to face?

● Will I be taught by full-time teachers, or by part timers with teaching experience, or by graduate students? If the latter, what steps are taken to ensure that they know their subject, have a good command of English, and are properly supervised?

Getting answers to these questions, even if you are not happy with the answers, will at least put you in touch with reality. And this will help you to be aware of and deal with mixed messages, which can otherwise severely stress and distress you.

Part of the art of being a successful student is learning to 'manage from underneath'. Even if they treat you at first as just one of the masses, and treat teaching as a matter of 'delivering' information to students and then testing them to see whether they have taken it in, try to induce them to adopt a more interactive way of working. Do this by taking them beyond the 'delivery and testing' pattern. Ask them questions (not just factual ones). Identify the skills that they're trying to teach you and ask them how well you're doing and how you could improve. Read 'around' the subject, write short notes on aspects that interest you, and ask them to look at these. Find puzzles and invent problems in the subject – e.g. where different writers disagree – try to solve them for yourself, and then ask your teacher's opinion: puzzles and problems will usually intrigue teachers and catch their imagination. Any of these could turn out to be a way of getting your teachers to take you seriously, and this will be the key to establishing yourself as a student and getting the most out of your higher education experience.

Finally, do your best to build a 'social network' for yourself. If you are like most people you will start by getting to know those who belong to the same minority as yourself. Your circle will probably extend naturally to include other members of whatever clubs and societies you join, and your neighbours in your hall of residence. Your social network will also be a mutual support network for you and others to call on when times are stressful.

It is very tempting to associate with people who are like you and who have the same interests as you. But I would urge you to branch out, to get out of your comfort zone. Take every opportunity that presents itself to get to know fellow students who are *not* like you. Having friends who are different from you broadens your horizons and can open doors to interesting, life-enhancing experiences.

Chapter 2

Intimidated by monster reading lists

Symptom

I feel really intimidated by the huge reading lists I've been issued with. We're given these lists of books and chapters and articles we're told to read before a class, and it's far too much to do: I just can't cope.

Diagnosis

You evidently haven't been told what the purpose of the 'huge' reading lists is, nor have you been taught how to use them discriminatingly.

Reading lists can be long because they are intended to be comprehensive and to equip you not only to take part in a class but also to write a first-class essay or exam answer on the subject. They can also be made long deliberately in order to provide choice, bearing in mind the difficulty of finding items in the library, and in the hope that different students will find different items, so between you all you will cover quite a lot of the list. Less commendably, a list may be long because it has been added to over the years but never 'weeded' to remove entries that are out of date or obsolete. And I've also heard it said that reading lists are usually too long because they are there to impress other teachers and validating committees, rather than to help students to learn.

Remedy

What you should do

Tell yourself: 'I am not obliged to read everything on the reading list before my class.' Say this half-a-dozen times, preferably aloud. Do this several times a day.

Think about the topic. If it isn't in the form of a question, turn it into one and ask yourself what information you need in order to answer it.

Get hold of three or four publications on the list – preferably ones that (a) are recent, and (b) seem to relate closely to the topic – and hunt through them for the information you reckon you need. You need something to contribute to the class. See if you can find four or five items. A good selection would comprise two interesting (e.g. surprising) pieces of knowledge, one difference of opinion between the writers you've encountered, one observation on the difficulty of finding the answer to the question, and one new question that you would like to bring to the class.

Some teachers are in the habit, when taking a class, of firing questions at students, thereby turning what should be an interesting discussion into an ordeal for some of you. If a question gets fired at you and you can't answer it, you need a helpful form of words for a reply. Something accurate and straightforward like 'My reading hasn't helped me on that point' should do. If you're asked 'What *have* you read?' you can say what you've read, and contribute one of the items you've prepared.

Keep your eye on the assessment ball. If you'll be sitting an unseen exam at the end of the year or the semester, or if you'll have to write an assessed essay on the subject in your own time, notice what publications the teacher refers to and what points he or she makes in the course of the discussion. Use these to guide your future reading.

And see the advice in Chapter 3.

What you should ask your teachers to do

Ask your teachers to give you much fuller and more realistic guidance on how to use reading lists. Ask them to distinguish between publications of central and peripheral interest, and to give you some guidance as to why a particular publication is important or useful to read, and which ones can be treated as alternatives. They should also weed out obsolete and unhelpful entries from their lists.

And ask your teachers to give you a demonstration of how to 'read' a reading list: ask them to go through a list in front of you, saying what each item brings to mind and identifying for you the clues in titles, dates, etc. as to the likely importance and value of each item. Moreover, every academic publication contains references, and by following up these references you can often track down useful nuggets of information and know-how. There's a skill to this 'tracking-down' process – it's a kind of detective work – so ask your teachers to demonstrate this skill to you too.

Chapter 3

Reading takes forever

Symptom

I'm a very slow reader, and I tend to get distracted when I'm reading. I have been known to fall asleep in the library. I find a lot of the stuff I have to read is very difficult to understand, and I have to read it several times to make sense of it.

Diagnosis

There are probably two main factors combining to bring about the stressful situation you find yourself in. One is the language that academic publications are written in; the other is the way you are approaching your reading, as though your task is to 'take in' everything in the book or whatever publication you are reading.

The language of academic subjects. Every academic subject has its own language, its 'academic-speak'. In some cases this is a technical jargon, with made-up words and expressions; in other cases the words and expressions used are ordinary English, often colloquial, but the meanings are unusual and special to the subject. It has also long been the fashion for academics to write in a complicated and convoluted way. As Anthony Giddens, former director of the London School of Economics, put it in an interview reported in the *Times Higher* on 28 May 2004:

> I'd spent most of my life writing books for an academic audience, and I used to make these more obscure than they needed to be because that sort of brought you esteem for your scholarship.

So academic language is difficult for the newcomer. It has to be mastered, and that takes time and effort.

Your approach to reading. Just about everyone who has made it into higher education takes it for granted that they know how to read. Basically, you begin at page one and continue reading until you get to the end, when you stop. Unfortunately, because of the sheer quantity and bulk of reading material, and its language, you stand very little chance of getting to the end of anything substantial inside a week or so unless you can concentrate exclusively on it.

When you take this approach you're operating on the 'absorption' model of reading: you're aiming to soak up great masses of stuff. But the human brain is not well suited to doing this. If you get distracted easily or fall asleep, what's happening is that your brain is sending you a message: 'You're giving me a really hard time! Do not make me do this!'

Remedy

What you should do

If you're getting the 'distress signal' message from your brain, pay attention to it. There are two things you can do to improve your reading strategy: change your idea of 'reading', and learn academic-speak as you would a foreign language.

Change your idea of 'reading'. Take a different model. Think of reading not as soaking up masses of stuff but as a treasure hunt. You're looking for the gems, the pearls, that you need. Bear in mind that unless the book was written specifically for students taking your course, it will contain a great deal of stuff that you do not need to know, especially if you are encountering it for the first time. So look for key terms – if you're reading because you have a class to prepare for or an essay to write, the assigned topic will supply these – and look for the author's conclusions. These won't necessarily be at the end of the book: they could be at the ends of individual chapters, or in the preface, the introduction, or an abstract. Track them down. If you want to find out how those conclusions were reached, you can then go on to do the necessary detective work. (People tend not to fall asleep when they're doing detective work!)

Learn academic-speak as you would a foreign language. The second thing you can do is to treat the particular brand of academic-speak you're faced with exactly as you would if it were a foreign language that you have to learn. So make a vocabulary book for yourself, with examples of the usage of the words and expressions you meet. You can develop this into a user manual for your course. And you can use the same approach for quantitative subjects too: it works for equations and diagrams in just the same way as for words and expressions in English.

Ideally, you will become fluent in the academic-speak of the subjects you're studying. If you're a native English speaker and learned French at school, you'll probably remember that when you started, if someone asked you a question in French you translated the question into English, worked out the answer in English, and then translated the answer into French. Then one day someone asked you a question in French and you answered straight off in French. That is precisely the level of fluency in academic-speak that you need to acquire.

What you should ask your teachers to do

Ask your teachers to give you a demonstration of how they themselves read. They can take a book or article and show you what strikes them as significant, and why, and what they pass over on a first reading. They can show you how they relate what they read to what they already know, and how they read critically, between the lines rather than taking the words on the page at face value.

If their subject is a quantitative one, they can similarly give a demonstration of how to 'read' a table of figures, a graph, a diagram or an equation.

Just as with a piece of writing, there are skills of questioning and inferring that they can illuminate and pass on to their students.

Chapter 4

On a different planet from your teachers

Symptom

There's something about one of my courses I'm just not getting. Most of my courses are quantitative ones, and we have problem exercises to do. But one of my courses, from another department, is very literature- and essay-based, and there's something about it that I'm just not getting. I feel as though I'm on a different planet from my teachers. It's very frustrating.

Diagnosis

Every academic course has a 'sub-plot'. You think you're there to learn the subject, but if you're to do well you must also learn something else, namely how your teachers think. It may well be that this is what's eluding you. Academics tend to be so deep in their subject, to live so closely within it, that they are not consciously aware of how they think.

Every discipline involves a particular perspective, a particular way of looking at the world. Thus, natural scientists see the world in terms of phenomena to be explained; people working in the social sciences and humanities mostly see it in terms of themes to be discussed and debates contributed to; and people working in practical and vocational disciplines see it in terms of issues to be dealt with and problems to be solved. It's most unlikely that your teachers will point this out to you. If you are taking courses from different departments you are particularly likely to be 'thrown' by differences in ways of thinking. For example, if you happen to be in the process of being trained as a problem-solver, you may find the 'thematic' mode of discourse very much a foreign language.

In the case of the social sciences and humanities there is an added twist. You may think you are there to study aspects of human behaviour or past events, but what you actually find yourself studying is *what has been written about* human behaviour or past events. If you don't show yourself to be sufficiently conversant with the writings, however well you know the 'real world' you won't gain rewards within the 'academic world'.

Another example of differences between disciplines is in the way they treat causation – i.e., cause and effect – and in the notions of explanation they employ. While there are some 'universals' – e.g., that an effect necessarily comes after its cause(s) and not before – there are significant differences between disciplines. Physicists reckon they have an explanation for a phenomenon when their observations of it are what they would expect from – and accordingly are consistent with – theory or their prior knowledge and understanding of mechanisms that are likely to be in operation. Historians aim to explain an event by asking whether one or more particular factors were 'responsible' for it: the explanations they offer often amount to nothing more than 'plausible accounts'. Academics in the humanities and social sciences are also prone to muddle up explanations and reasons, which exist in their heads, with mechanisms and processes that exist in the real world: look out for references to 'reasons' why something did or did not happen.

There is one thing that academics of all disciplines tend to have in common, however: they can shuttle very rapidly between two levels, the level of 'principle' and the level of 'detail', the general and the particular.

They make an observation and immediately ask how it fits into the big picture, and what its wider – general – implications are. Offered a new theory, they work from the general to the particular, asking what particular observations could be made that would test its validity. This habit of shuttling up and down between the general and the particular, of working from theory to observation and back again, of shifting focus between principle and detail, is the academic's way of 'making sense'.

Remedy

What you should do
Bear in mind that you are in the business of learning how your teachers think. A few students manage to do this intuitively, by a kind of osmosis, but for most it is more difficult, especially if they are being trained in another, different way of thinking.

Be alert for signs that reveal their mindset, their way of looking at the world. In particular, notice their language. When people use language, they do so to express their thoughts, so the kind of language they use is a good guide to the kind of thinking they do. If they often refer to actual phenomena, or to a theme or debate, or to a problem or issue, their language is revealing their mindset.

Notice how your teachers use colloquial, as well as technical, specialist language. Whatever their language, you need to become fluent in it. In effect, you need to learn to speak to each of your teachers in the language they understand.

Pay particular attention to the language they use when talking or writing about cause and effect. This will often imply that they have models of explanation in mind, but it will be a rare event if they make these explicit to you.

Look out too for academics shuttling between 'high-level' general principle and 'ground-level' details. Words like 'background', 'context', 'overview', 'theme', 'perspective' and 'principle' are indicators of high-level thinking. 'Case', 'case study', 'test', 'experiment', 'practice', 'observation', 'detail' and 'particular' are indicators of 'ground-level' thinking.

What you should ask your teachers to do

Before academics can communicate their ways of looking at the world to students, they need to become aware of them themselves. They could make a start on this by noticing how their colleagues working in other disciplines operate and by thinking about what it means to see the world as a physicist, historian, economist, psychologist, lawyer, engineer or whatever: what registers with them, what they take for granted, what questions they ask, and what methods, tools and techniques they use to interrogate the world.

Help to nudge them in this direction by doing your own noticing and asking them questions. Ask them too about how the thinking behind your various courses differs and how those courses are related to one another. (They may have given little or no thought to this.)

Chapter 5

Knee-deep in notes

Symptom

What do I do with all these notes I've made? I've been making notes conscientiously when I'm reading. I've produced vast amounts of notes and it has taken me ages. I tried using highlighter but found I ended up highlighting almost everything. Now exams are in sight and I feel I ought to be using my notes, but I don't know how.

Diagnosis

Many teachers tell students that they should make notes on what they read. However, they do so without giving advice on how and when to make notes, or indeed on how to make useful, high-quality, notes. And many students make notes unbidden – they take it for granted that that is what they ought to be doing – and give no thought to the question of quality until very late in the day.

The root of the problem here, I suspect, is that you're making notes when you're reading a book or article for the first time. And on that first reading, it's difficult to know what is relevant to the task in hand – e.g. writing an essay – and what isn't. Not having any criteria of relevance to apply, you are tempted to include anything you think might possibly be relevant, 'just in case'. If you've gone in for highlighting, I expect your pages are like many I've seen, covered in colour, sometimes a veritable rainbow of pink, orange, yellow and green.

There's also the matter of the quality of your notes. If you have merely been copying from the publication, you've been doing nothing more than acting as an inefficient copying machine. Apart from (somewhat blindly and indiscriminately) selecting what you're going to copy, there's nothing of *you* in your notes: you have not contributed any thought to them. And you didn't have the experience of thinking about your notes as you made them, which would help you to remember them. If you've been thinking of your notes as a kind of 'security blanket' – just having them makes you feel safe – think again: any sense of security you get from poor-quality notes has no substance: it is an illusion.

In the run-up to exams, I have frequently been asked by students 'How should I use these notes that I've made?' I have mostly found it very difficult to give an encouraging answer. The truth is that their notes are often worthless. The material hasn't been digested; it isn't in a form that lends itself to incorporation in exam answers and the valuable bits are like needles in a haystack. The more capable students, on looking at their notes, do appreciate that they have to go back to the original source, but by that point time may be running out.

Remedy

What you should do
The main piece of advice that I have for you is this: *Don't make notes on a first reading!* Follow the 'treasure hunt' advice in Chapter 3: scan for key terms and conclusions, and when you come across something that looks as though it might be interesting, stick a Post-it on the page to serve as a bookmark and

carry on scanning. Save making notes for the time when you know what parts of the publication are relevant and accordingly valuable.

When you find yourself tempted to make detailed notes, look ahead to the possibility that you might be setting yourself up to encounter the 'huge stacks of notes at revision time' problem. Forestall that problem by asking yourself how you would be likely to use a particular note that you're making: if you don't get a convincing answer stop what you're doing.

If you really want to remember stuff that you come across in books, etc., don't merely copy it out: *use it* in some way. Use it to 'cross-check' lecture notes that you've made, i.e. to see if what you've been told in lectures tallies with what's in the books. Or use it to solve problems, or to construct outline ('bullet point') or model essays or answers to past exam questions. The crucial thing is to *do something with it*, so you engage with it actively, not passively.

What you should ask your teachers to do

Your teachers should never content themselves with merely conveying information to you: they should always say *why* that information is significant, show you what can be done with it, and demonstrate how it relates to other information, concepts, theories, etc. If they don't do this without prompting, prompt them. By so doing they will school you in making notes that are 'integrated', that are linked together, and consequently much easier to use at exam time than those that are merely an accumulation of extracts from the literature.

Chapter 6

Suffering from writer's block

Symptom

I suffer from writer's block. I can't get started on writing essays. Sometimes I just sit and stare at the screen for hours. I very often feel I've got to do more reading before I can start. I get told to stop procrastinating and pull my socks up.

Diagnosis

So-called 'writer's block' is not restricted to students: it's a common affliction among professional writers too. There may well be some psychological factors operating here. Perhaps a bit of you really does not want to be doing this piece of writing, and you're doing more reading as a 'displacement activity', to put off starting. Perhaps your subconscious mind is sorting out what you've read and 'processing' it. This does work for some people (especially experienced writers), but it takes time, and the more anxious you are the less likely it is to happen. Being told to stop procrastinating won't help you in the slightest.

It could also be that you have tried to start writing too soon. Every task expands to fill the time available, and essay-writing is no exception. If you start before you feel you really have to, you may well experience difficulty in focusing on your task: you simply don't yet care enough about it.

Along with any psychological factors, however, there are likely to be one or two very practical and extremely common obstacles hindering you. One – the main one – is that you simply do not know any techniques for getting started: no one has taken the trouble to teach them to you. And lacking any advice to the contrary, the technique that you probably do adopt is to try to put perfectly formed sentences onto the page from the very start. This course of action is bound to lead to frustration, because you are trying to do two incompatible things simultaneously: you're trying to brainstorm and to edit at the same time.

Remedy

What you should do

To begin, consider the task in front of you. Before you can produce an essay, or indeed a dissertation or a piece of writing for publication, you have to do some thinking. It is the experience of many academics – probably the great majority, I suspect – that writing plays an important part in their thinking process. This 'early stage' writing does not consist of producing perfectly formed sentences: it consists of 'rough work', making notes. It's only in the later stages of editing and producing a final draft that the writer thinks about presentation, crafting the piece to appeal to the reader. This is a good scheme for you to follow.

The question 'How do I get started?' is thus replaced by another: 'How do I make useful notes that will aid my thinking?' Here is a formula for doing this, a formula for 'structured brainstorming', which I have seen many students follow, with remarkably good results. It starts from the premise that you have been assigned a topic for your essay. The formula involves thinking about, and making rough notes on, the following:

- Background/overview/context
- Interpretation, of the topic and the individual words and phrases that comprise it (including any instruction, such as 'discuss' and 'critically evaluate . . .')
- Methodology, the reasoning you will employ
- Materials, the documentary and other sources you will use.

Background/overview/context. Ask yourself: Why is this subject interesting? Does it relate to a current debate among academics or to a topical issue? Is there a 'big picture' that it fits into? (If you subsequently begin your essay with this, your teachers will usually be impressed to see that you are aware of it and have given thought to it.)

Interpretation. It is absolutely crucial (a) that you ask what *meanings* you should assign to each of the individual words and phrases that make up the topic, and (b) that you look for *and challenge* any wording that has an 'underlying message', a statement or instruction that is implicit – 'sneaked in', so to speak – rather than made explicit.

Under 'meanings', look out in particular for:

(1) Words that different writers use to mean different things. (It would be sensible to show your reader that you are aware of these different usages rather than opting for just one without saying why you are doing that.)

(2) Abstract and technical terms: these may need translating.

(3) Colloquial – 'ordinary' – language and figures of speech, such as metaphors: these certainly will need translating into more precise terms.

'Underlying messages' that you should identify and challenge will include:

(1) Presumptions, e.g. the presumption that something exists (a purported fact) or is 'a good thing'.

(2) Generalizations: these are a form of presumption but worth distinguishing as a separate category. For example, if you are asked 'Why did Latin America default on its debts in the 1930s?', you should notice the presumption, the underlying message, that Latin America can be treated as a monolithic whole. You aren't explicitly being asked to challenge this, but you must do so if you are to get a good mark: you must distinguish between the different countries (or some of them) that

comprise Latin America, because each has its own particular record of treatment of its debts in that period.

(3) Words that include or exclude or quantify: these too may need to be challenged. If little words like 'all' or 'only' appear in the topic, to get good marks your essay may need to show that the topic is true of 'some', or 'others', or is true under some circumstances but not others.

(4) Time-related words and expressions. These may specify dates, time spans, frequencies, etc: 'has/have been', 'has/have/will become', 'today', 'currently', 'still', 'rarely', 'sometimes', 'frequently', 'often', 'always'. Or they may specify time-related processes, such as 'development', 'evolution' and sequences and successions of events or situations.

(5) Wording that conveys a claim, assertion, judgement, opinion or an assumption of some kind. You should bring these out – make them explicit – if they are hidden, and always test or challenge them.

(6) Wording that denotes cause and effect, like 'was significant', 'was responsible for', 'could not have taken place without'. It will usually be a good idea to cover in your essay some or all of the following: other possible causal factors, mechanisms and processes that could have operated, surrounding circumstances and conditions, and 'counter-factuals', alternative (imagined) effects that might have come about but did not.

(7) Wording that – usually misleadingly – conveys degree or distance, such as 'How far . . .?' and 'To what extent . . .?' If you're asked in a cause-and-effect question 'How far/to what extent was X responsible for . . .?', you should interpret this as a question about X *in relation to other factors*, so your essay must deal with these other factors as well as X.

Methodology. Most essay topics come in one of two forms: a question, which you are required to answer, or a statement (proposition), which you are required to discuss or comment on. Virtually all statements can be expressed as – turned into – questions, either by slightly altering the wording or pre-fixing it with the words 'Is it valid to say that . . .' and tacking a question mark on the end. Your methodology is your way of getting from that question to your answer: the method(s) and/or principles that you will use. Of course, you 'get' from question to answer by a process of reasoning, so your methodology is in effect a toolkit for reasoning. And a good essay will set out the reasoning by which you have got from question to answer, so it will take the reader along that same path. (If you're studying any subjects that involve solving problems, you should be familiar with this process: it's analogous to the process by which you get from problem to solution.)

If all this sounds a bit abstract, here's how to make it concrete. First, express your essay topic as a question, if it isn't in that form already. (Never, ever, set out merely to 'write about X' or to 'look at Y'.) Once you have that question, ask yourself another: 'How can I tell (discover, find out) what the answer is? When you have your answer to this second question, you have identified your methodology.

Most methodologies take the form of a sequence of steps. Typically the first step will be to elaborate on the subject: you say more about it, identify its significant features, or whatever. Your next step might be to analyse it, or 'compare and contrast' it with something else, extrapolate trends, offer alternative views of it, whatever is appropriate. If that step generates 'findings' of some kind, you can then go on to the next, which would be to comment on the significance of those findings. The range of possibilities is great, so it's difficult and not very helpful to try to go further and offer a more detailed 'recipe'. But if you have never before thought about methodology when writing an essay, try it now: by focusing your mind on things you can actively do, it offers you a way of getting past writer's block.

Materials. All academic writing involves making use of documentary and other materials. These may be publications drawn from the academic literature, or from the professional literature if there is one. You may be using formal publications (e.g. statutes and law reports) and/or official and other data sources (e.g. census reports). Depending on your subject, you may get information through other communication channels too. There's no need to make heavy weather of this: my point is simply that you will usually find it useful to think in advance about the materials you'll be using. It will prompt you to check whether there is anything you've left out and whether you are making sufficient use of the academic literature to satisfy your teachers. (This is often a danger if they are individuals who see their subject not as human behaviour or past events but *what has been written about* human behaviour or past events: see Chapter 4.) Remember that one of the things teachers look for when reading your essays is evidence that you have read widely and, of course, thought about what you have read.

To sum up. A good way of getting started on an essay – and getting past any block that you might have come up against – is to make rough notes on background, overview, context; interpretation; methodology; and materials. And here's an added bonus. When you've got those notes, boil them down into three or four sentences. Now add another, beginning 'In this essay I shall . . .' and outlining the series of steps your methodology will take you through. Hey presto! You now have your introduction to your essay. It really is as straightforward as that.

What you should ask your teachers to do

In a nutshell, your teachers should encourage you to follow the above procedure when embarking on writing an essay. In particular, they should encourage you to think about methodology. Most academics could do a great deal more in this vein, not least by demonstrating their own methodology, their own reasoning processes, to their students. If they don't do this voluntarily, ask them to do it for you. It would go a very long way to raise the quality of learning in UK universities.

Chapter 7

Mystified by essay topics

Essays: I don't understand what I'm expected to do. What do the instructions – Discuss! Critically evaluate! Explain! and so on – mean? I'm really confused. And my teachers say things like 'I want to see a strong argument': what does that mean? I usually end up trying to write everything I know about the subject, but obviously that's not what I should be doing.

Diagnosis

Your confusion is entirely understandable. It results, in my opinion, from the fact that your teachers themselves are unclear about exactly what they want you to do. Some of them make their lack of clarity perfectly plain by merely asking you to 'write about' a subject rather than assigning a concrete topic to you, or by setting exam questions that consist of a direct question (ending with a question mark) followed by 'Discuss': anyone with half a brain knows that what a question calls for is an answer, not a discussion, so the instruction 'Discuss' is not only superfluous but will confuse the examinee. Confusion on the part of academics is also apparent in their tendency to use the same instruction to mean different things: examples of this are given below.

Asking you a question and then telling you to produce an argument is also guaranteed to confuse you. Asking you a question sets your mind working 'forwards' from question to answer, a perfectly logical way of working. Telling you to produce an argument suggests to you (perhaps subconsciously) that you should start with your answer, which is the reverse of logical. It's like telling a joke starting with the punchline: what on earth do you say next? You are distracted from your task of interpreting the question, and you are put in a position where you are scrabbling around for evidence to back up your argument: this is likely to lead you to overlook evidence that does *not* back it up.

Remedy

What you should do

If you are asked to 'write about' a subject, ask your teacher for a proper topic: a direct question or a statement (which you can then turn into a direct question yourself).

If you are asked to 'produce an argument', interpret that as a request for reasoning. There is good authority for doing this. Anthony Weston, in his classic little book *A Rulebook for Arguments* (3rd edition), writes: 'In this book, "to give an argument" means to offer a set of reasons or evidence in support of a conclusion.' And indeed, his book is all about reasoning. In my experience, it is rare for students to be penalized for offering reasoning in an essay: cogent reasoning is (fortunately) likely to be rewarded.

If your teacher does insist that he or she requires an argument, add to your opening paragraph a sentence beginning: 'It will be shown that ...' That should do the trick for all but the most unreasonable academic.

What to do about all those obscure instructions? As I noted above, they can often be interpreted to mean several different things. You can usually work out which one you should use from the subject matter, the content of the topic.

For example, if the instruction is 'Explain', that could mean: (1) 'Say clearly what is meant by . . .'; *or* (2) 'Tell the story of how X came about'; *or* (3) 'Show how causes combine to bring about certain effects'; *or* (4) 'State the reasons that someone had for behaving in the way they did'. If the subject matter is a technical term, you need interpretation no. 1; if it is an event or situation, you need no. 2; if it is a cause-and-effect relationship you need no. 3; and if it is someone's behaviour you need no. 4.

'Describe' could mean: (1) List the significant characteristics of the subject (in which case you will have to decide which characteristics to regard as significant ones); *or* (2) Say in addition to no. 1 *why* you consider these characteristics to be significant; *or* (3) Say in addition to 1 and 2 how these characteristics are interconnected, e.g. how if one is present others will be. So how should you proceed? Look to your subject for clues. To take a simple example, if you are required to describe a structure and how it works, you would not be expected to describe aspects of the structure that don't have a bearing on how it works.

'Analyse' could mean: (1) Describe in detail; *or* (2) Break down into component parts; *or* (3) Show how causes combine to bring about certain effects. You will get clues as to which approach is appropriate from looking at the subject, not from worrying over what is meant by 'analyse'.

'Compare and contrast' could mean: (1) List similarities and differences; *or* (2) Formulate and apply criteria that can be used for comparison; *or* (3) Say in addition to no. 1 and/or no. 2 how the similarities and differences come about. Once again, clues as to how you should proceed will be found in the nature of the things to be compared and contrasted rather than in the instruction.

As for 'Discuss', 'Discuss critically', 'Comment on the view that . . .', and 'Do you agree?', these are all highly vague and unspecific instructions. What you must do, accordingly, is take your cue from your interpretation of the statement to be discussed, etc. (See the section on 'interpretation' in chapter 6.) Similarly with 'Evaluate' and 'Critically evaluate': these instructions imply that there is something in the statement that you should offer a judgement on. It will usually be a claim, opinion or assertion, but could also be an implicit assumption or a piece of reasoning, the validity of which you could challenge.

What you should ask your teachers to do

Your teachers should be aware that asking students to do more than 'write about' a subject is poor academic practice. In the interest of good education, they owe it to you and your fellow students to give you a proper topic: a direct question or a statement (which you can then turn into a direct question yourself). Ask for this if you aren't given it. And in the interest of fairness, they should demonstrate to you, with worked examples, ways of responding to essay instructions. Not to do this is to condemn you to playing a game, the rules of which have been concealed from you. So ask for this demonstration too.

Chapter 8

Demoralized by 'negative feedback'[1]

Symptom

'The feedback I get on my work is really unhelpful. I get essays back with the comment that I need to improve my essay structure, or to say more about X, or 'you haven't put enough thought into this', or sometimes even 'good work', but I've no idea what I need to do to get better marks. And it can take three or four weeks to get an essay back. It's very demoralizing. '

Diagnosis

Student dissatisfaction about the quality of the feedback they get has been very common at UK universities. The Dearing Committee noted in 1997 that 'fewer than half the students responding to our survey were satisfied with the feedback they got from staff about their work'.[2] The situation has changed very little since then: the 2006 National Student Survey found that around half of UK students were not satisfied with the feedback they received.[3]

Not knowing what to do to raise the standard of your work reduces learning to a process of trial and error: you're forever trying new ways in the hope that you'll get better marks, and looking for clues from the marks that other students get. After a while you get disoriented (submitting work but getting little or no constructive feedback amounts to a kind of sensory deprivation); you get disheartened (you're playing a game where you don't know what you have to do to score); and you lose patience. All perfectly understandable, I think.

Sometimes you may be asked to submit a specialized piece of writing, like a book review, without having been taught how to create it. If you don't get constructive feedback on your efforts, you will never learn. I have known new students on a master's' course to be asked to write a book review so that their teachers could see what knowledge and understanding of the subject they already possessed, but then receive comments that were highly critical and not at all constructive: the reviews had evidently been marked as if the real purpose of the exercise was assessment, not diagnosis and learning. Not only did the students feel discouraged and demoralized: they felt that they had been treated unfairly too.

Remedy

What you should do

In these circumstances, you have to take the initiative. I don't underestimate the difficulty of doing this. The ethos of the UK university system is pretty much that students take what they are given. You're at the bottom of a power structure, and students are there for only a limited period while staff are relatively permanent and so have been there longer – in some cases much longer – than you. And it certainly isn't in your interest to antagonize your teachers. You want their goodwill as far as possible.

So what can you do? One approach is to mount a campaign: to mobilize the power that you and your fellow-students have as a collective. Get together and write down the problems you are having. Create a document, with examples of unhelpful comments and of helpful ones (if any) as well.

The latter are valuable because they demonstrate what is possible, what can be done, and they also demonstrate that you appreciate it when your teachers do give you helpful comments.

All these examples constitute evidence to use in your campaign. Make it clear in your document how damaging and demoralizing unhelpful and late comments are to you. And state clearly what it is that you want.

Make use of existing avenues to present your case: student representatives on departmental bodies, staff–student committees, departmental tutor, head of department. And enlist the support of people who are sympathetic to your cause: ask them to have a private word with those who are not disposed to be sympathetic.

If you adopt this approach, working through established channels, you are behaving responsibly. But sometimes behaving responsibly does not produce results. At such times, you have to consider whether you are prepared to go further. If you are, let it be known that you are prepared to take the matter outside the department. Most academics will find it highly embarrassing if deans, managers, pro-vice-chancellors and other academics become involved in teaching issues: the general expectation within the academic world is that such issues will be dealt with within the department concerned. So they will try quite hard to head you off, and are likely to take you and your campaign more seriously if they see that you are serious. It will be even more embarrassing if the issue comes to the attention of higher education bodies outside the university and to prospective students and their parents. But do what you can to avoid matters reaching that point: try all other avenues first.

As an individual, you have to adopt a different approach. Essentially, you have a task: to elicit useful feedback from your teacher. There are a number of things you can do.

When you get an essay or other piece of work back with little or nothing in the way of helpful comment, go and see the person who marked it (make an appointment, or call in during an 'office hour'), taking the essay and comments with you, of course. It will help to have thought in advance about precisely what you will say. I suggest something on these lines: 'I'm really interested in this subject and would like to do well in it, so I was disappointed in the mark I got for this essay. Could you please give me some guidance as to what I could have done to get a better mark?' If this is not productive, try some prompts: 'Was my introduction OK? Was my conclusion wrong, or did I leave anything out? Did I do the reading I should have, or read widely enough? Do you think I answered the question? Did you think there was something about the structure of the essay that wasn't right? Is there something about this subject that I'm not getting?'

Sometimes you might call on a teacher but find that his or her mind is elsewhere, or there may be a long queue of people behind you. Don't be shy about asking 'Would it be better if I came back tomorrow?' – but don't accept a delay longer than a couple of days: 'I'd like to get this sorted while it's still fresh in my mind.' As a student, there to learn, and paying fees for the privilege, it is your right to ask questions of your teachers, and you should feel free to exercise that right.

Something else that you can usefully do is to dig out some past exam questions and prepare outline answers in bullet-point form. Then try these out on your teacher. You should be able to get a bullet-point answer – word-processed, of course – onto a single sheet of paper, and it will take only a couple of minutes for your teacher to run his or her eyes over the page and spot errors, omissions, etc. By adopting this tactic you are making only minimal demands on your teacher's time and effort, and this will undoubtedly be appreciated.

It may be that your teachers are requiring you to submit very little work for marking (it's a way of limiting the demands on their time). This is a real danger for you: when you face exams at the end of the year you have very little idea of the standards that will be applied. In these circumstances do yourself a favour and try the bullet-point tactic. It could be a real life-saver.

It is just possible, however, that your request will be refused on the grounds that 'If I do it for you I'll have to do it for everybody'. My view is that it demands very little time and they should indeed do it for everybody. But if you get this response get into campaigning mode (see the suggestions above).

If, like the students in the case I mentioned above, you have been asked to submit a specialized piece of writing, like a book review, without having been taught how to create it, and then don't get constructive comments on it, you should feel entirely justified in pursuing your teachers to elicit useful feedback. Again, get together with other students if that is what is needed. If you too have received unhelpful and discouraging comments on something like a book review, put these comments in context by asking yourself the following questions:

- Had I actually been taught how to carry out the task I was given?
- Did I have other books to compare with the one I was asked to review?
- Was I advised about using published book reviews as models, given that book reviews are generally written by authorities on the subject, a category to which I don't belong?

If your answers are no, no, no, it should be clear to you how the dice were loaded against you from the start. You may still be smarting at the unfairness of it, but it should be apparent that your marks are an indication not of your intellectual ability but of how badly your teachers prepared you for the task they set you. Do go through the comments you've received just in case there is some potentially useful advice in there. Then you might like to take the paper that they are written on – if they came by email make a printout – and tear it into small pieces. Experience shows this to be very therapeutic!

What you should ask your teachers to do

The above suggestions are all to do with asking and prompting your teachers to fulfil their responsibility to give you constructive and timely comments on your work. Take every opportunity to encourage your department to monitor how well teachers fulfil that responsibility.

And ask your teachers to refrain from setting you and your fellow-students tasks that, in the light of your experience and the point in the course you are at, cannot be of any significant benefit to you. If an opportune moment arises, you might also invite them to imagine what effect on you their comments on your work will have, and avoid making any that can only demoralize you.

Chapter 9

Let down by poor spelling

Symptom

We're expected to do a lot of writing, but my spelling is poor and even with a spell-checker I make mistakes. Am I dyslexic? PS: I'm a very slow reader too.

Diagnosis

I can't tell you whether or not you have a physiological condition that qualifies as dyslexia and/or makes writing and reading unusually problematic for you, but I can tell you that for English speakers difficulty in spelling words correctly can have a number of contributory causes. One is the fact that English is not a phonetic language, so once you get beyond c-a-t you can't work out how to spell a word from the sounds that you utter when you speak it. (Amazingly, phonics is currently at the heart of the UK's literacy strategy.) Another is the way that spelling is and has been taught in UK schools. When I ask university students what recollection they have of being taught to spell, nine times out of ten they respond by telling me about their memories not of being taught but of being *tested*.

For people who have difficulty with spelling, memories of childhood spelling tests are invariably traumatic. Sarcastic teachers, mocking or pitying schoolmates, inability to eat or sleep because of an impending test ... the spelling regime in many schools is for a significant number of children a highly effective way not of teaching spelling but of installing a phobia about it! Ten, 15, 20 years on, you sit down to write, want to use a word that you're not sure how to spell, and immediately the phobia kicks in: you're hit by feelings of fear, incompetence and humiliation. Not a good bit of baggage to be carrying.

By the way, if you are one of those gifted people who think very quickly, whose minds 'race', you may spell words incorrectly for a reason that has nothing to do with a disability or inability. What's happening is that as you are writing or typing a word, your mind is actually on the next word but 10 (or thereabouts). You are liable to spell a word incorrectly simply because you are not paying attention to it.

Many students who have difficulties with spelling, and reckon themselves to be slow or very slow readers, jump to the conclusion that they have a dyslexic condition. They shouldn't, and – if tempted – neither should you. Spelling has been badly taught in UK schools probably since it was standardized in the eighteenth century, and *everyone* reads slowly when struggling with academic-speak for the first time, as I pointed out in Chapter 3. So literally the last thing you should do is blame yourself for your difficulties.

Remedy

What you should do

There is more than one way in which you can learn to spell a word. The most effective, in my experience, starts with seeing that word spelled correctly and takes you, via a series of steps, to the point where you can recollect accurately – without help – how to spell it for yourself. What you are recollecting is how the word looks, so you are *visualizing* it: seeing it 'in your mind's eye'.[4]

You can train yourself to visualize. Here's an example. I'm using the word 'beautiful', but when trying the exercise for yourself pick any word that causes you trouble; just take care that you begin with it spelled correctly! The process works best if you have a friend to take you through it, but it's perfectly feasible to do it on your own. For best results choose a time and place where you're reasonably relaxed.

Step 1. Look up your difficult word in a dictionary and write it down in large letters on a piece of A4 paper on its side ('landscape' mode), like this:

beautiful

Step 2. Split the word up into small chunks, in whatever way you find satisfactory, putting hyphens between the chunks (I could have split 'beautiful' into 'be-au-ti-ful', but that didn't appeal to me) and write it out again on a piece of A4, like this:

b-eau-ti-ful

Step 3. Now take some coloured markers and write it out once more (this is the last time!), using a different coloured marker for each chunk and leaving out the hyphens. Because this book is printed only in black and white, I've not been able to use different colours for my example (if you like, you can colour in the different chunks, using different colours, for yourself), but you can see how it works:

b eau ti ful

Step 4. Relax! This is going to be fun. Hold the sheet of paper in front of you and look at the word for 10 or 15 seconds or so. Then turn it face down, look upwards – preferably towards a blank piece of wall – and 'see' the word; picture it in your mind's eye. You probably won't see it correctly the first time: that doesn't matter.

Step 5. After a few seconds of picturing the word, look down towards the sheet of paper again. Turn the sheet upwards and look at the colourful word for 10 or 15 seconds once more: notice the chunks one by one, shifting your gaze consciously from left to right. Then again, as in Step 4, turn the sheet face down, look up at the blank wall and picture the word in your mind's eye. You might get a better result (many people do, especially if they are right-handed) if you're looking upwards and to the left rather than straight ahead.

Steps 6 to n (however many steps it takes). Repeat Step 5 a few times. What will happen after a few repetitions is that your mental picture and the actual colourful word on the page become 'synchronized': you won't need to consciously check whether they are the same; you just *know* they are. At this point in the process people invariably relax: the tension visibly leaves their bodies, their shoulders drop, they often flop in their chair and smile.

Step n+1. Without looking at any of the pieces of paper you've used up to now, take a clean piece of paper, look upwards and see the word in your mind's eye, and – without taking time to think – write down the word. Now check it against your original version to see if it's correct. If it is, congratulate yourself! If you've got it wrong, take a breather and then repeat Step 5 a few more times.

If there's someone with you, they can help. They should ask you to place the sheet of paper face down, look upwards and see the word in your mind's eye, and read aloud the letters of the word. If you've got it wrong, they'll tell you. In that case, again, take a breather and then repeat the process.

Step n+2. Without looking at any of the pieces of paper you've used up to now, take a fresh piece of paper, look upwards and see the word in your mind's eye, and – again without taking time to think – write down the letters of the word *in reverse order*, i.e. starting with the last and working backwards. Now check what you've written against the correct version to see if your reverse-order spelling is correct. If it is, congratulate yourself again! (If you've got it wrong, take a breather and again repeat Step 5 a few more times.)

If you've got the reverse-order spelling correct, that is the absolute clincher. You can only have done that by 'seeing' the word in your mind's eye, i.e. by visualizing it.

I emphasize here the 'doing without thinking' for this reason: students in higher education often make a mess of the visualizing process because they are trying to think at the same time. They are trying to link the word with its sound, or they are inventing little word games. I know someone who chooses to recollect the correct spelling of 'predilection' (as opposed to 'predeliction') by reminding himself that it is an 'Old Macdonald' word: the vowels go e-i-e-i-o. If you are inventing such word games when you are trying the above exercise, it will interfere with your ability to visualize. If you catch yourself doing it, stop!

As for the remedy for 'slow reading', please read again the advice I gave in Chapter 3: treat reading as a 'treasure hunt' and not an exercise in absorbing masses of information.

What you should ask your teachers to do

Your present teachers weren't appointed to their posts to teach you to spell, and indeed some of them are not proficient in spelling. So you cannot realistically expect them to provide help. If your institution has a study-skills unit, by all means approach it and see what help is on offer.

Chapter 10

Stumped for a dissertation subject

Symptom

I've got a dissertation to do but no idea what to do it on, and if I don't submit my title next week I'm in trouble.

Diagnosis

It sounds as though you haven't been given much help by your teachers on this so far.

Your summing-up of your situation reveals a need for some clear thinking. The very notion of 'having a dissertation to do' is one that requires some clarification, some 'unpacking'. So let's be precise here. You have to *write* a dissertation, and you have to *submit* it no later than a particular date. And every worthwhile dissertation I've ever seen is 'on' a project of some kind: that's to say, your dissertation presents the findings of a piece of work that you've carried out, discusses their significance, and offers the conclusions that you draw from them.

Remedy

What you should do

Let's have a restatement of your situation. You have to do a project, but as yet you don't know what form your project should take, or what to take as its subject.

What grabs you? Most people start from a general idea about the subject they want to tackle. They say things like 'It would be interesting to look at the Human Rights Act 1998' or 'I'd like to write about the Crimean war'. Statements like these are not specific enough to get you going – they say nothing about the approach that you're going to adopt – but they do give you a starting point. What will *your* starting point be?

The formal requirements for your dissertation will impose some limitations on your choice of subject. You will certainly be required to produce a dissertation that is your own work, and it would be sensible not to take a subject that you know someone else has taken unless your approach would be different and/or you have good grounds for thinking that you would come up with different results and conclusion. Your subject does not need to be one that no one else anywhere has ever tackled before, and your dissertation ought not be judged on whether it makes an original contribution to knowledge (that's for a PhD), but in practice it is almost certainly worth trying to find a combination of subject and approach that breaks some new ground. Below are some questions to get you thinking along those lines. At this stage, don't worry about how to choose a single subject: concentrate for now on drawing up a shortlist of possibles. Anything from two to five will be a good number.

- Is there something that you've come across in one of your taught courses that you didn't have time to explore properly but would like to know more about? Have you ever asked a teacher a question and not been satisfied with the answer? Now's your chance to see if you can put together a better one. Checking out past exam papers might give you an idea or two.

- What's currently happening in your field of study? In most fields there's usually something new or recent to be investigated. Is there a new book or article with new ideas, the implications of which you would like to explore? Is there a disagreement, with protagonists expressing different points of view? This offers scope for exploring how it is possible for different views to be held and the possibility of reconciling them. Has a new theory been published, one that you could test? Has a new technique become available, one which you could compare with or apply alongside existing techniques? If a new product has become available, could you explore its properties and evaluate its usefulness?

- Has a new source of data become available, offering a rich vein of material for analysis? Do you have contacts outside university giving you access to materials to which you could apply methodologies that you have learned?

- Has someone published a case study that it would be interesting to replicate in a different context, allowing you to compare its findings with your own and to test – and possibly refine – their methodology?

- Is there some literature in your field that you are critical of, or a train of thought you would like to pursue? Do you feel that you have something to contribute to a current debate? Or is there a gap of some kind that you think you could fill? (A gap by itself may not be very inspiring, however: see if you can formulate a question or puzzle that would help you to fill it.)

- Do you have some personal experience that you would like to draw on? This is legitimate, and will certainly help you to meet any requirement to do with originality, but there are traps that you must avoid. You must not merely give an account of your experience but place it in the context of other studies and/or theories. And you must avoid being judgmental: confine your judgments to your discussion and conclusions, and, if you can, clarify the values on which they are based. It's a good idea to take other people's experiences as your subject, and draw on your own to give you insights into their experiences.

- If you're an international student in a social science field, would it be interesting – and feasible – to make a comparative study between your home country and the UK, or to investigate a UK-centred subject that would generate useful lessons that you could take home with you?

Some words of warning. Avoid subjects set in the future, like 'What will happen if/when ...?' The future cannot be investigated, and although you may be able to get somewhere by extrapolating into the future you'll get very few if any marks for speculating about it.

And don't let your supervisor talk you into taking on a subject that you are not comfortable with. That is a sure-fire way of increasing the stress that you're under. Supervisors often have their own agenda and some are not at all good at putting themselves in a student's shoes. Get as much informed advice as you can (or can accommodate: too much advice can be very inhibiting) but at the end of the day trust your own instincts and make your own decision.

At the end of this exercise you should have a shortlist of two to five possible subjects. You should also be thinking at this stage about the form that your project could take. For example, it could be a project to find the answer to a research question, to test a theory or hypothesis, to evaluate an action or proposal, or to formulate a critique. It could be practical, involving field or laboratory work, or it could be library-based 'desk research'.

Once you have your shortlist, you can start thinking about which to choose. Here is a checklist of questions to ask about each one:

Is your subject specific enough?
If you have identified a possible subject in general terms, you are probably thinking of it in quite 'woolly' language. You need to express it in specific, 'concrete' terms. So translate all colloquial and abstract words into down-to-earth language: describe your subject in terms that will enable anyone to recognize it when they see it.

Is your subject narrow enough?
Your subject must have 'boundaries'. This might involve limiting it to one or two particular case studies, geographical areas, historical periods, organizations, physical phenomena, writers, or socio-economic groups, for example. Bear in mind the unavoidable trade-off between breadth and depth: the broader your subject, the shallower your project must be; and the deeper you go, the narrower you have to draw your boundaries.

Have you a clear aim?
It will help you to have a clear aim: get it clear in your mind what it is that you want to learn about your subject.

Have you a feasible approach?
Identifying a feasible approach to your subject requires you to ensure that you have a methodology that will enable you to achieve your aim, the materials to which you can apply your methodology, and the personal resources (such as time and ability) that you will need.

Can you envisage arriving at an interesting conclusion?
It will be very helpful if you can visualize, in at least a broad outline, an interesting conclusion that you might come to, and get some indication from your supervisor that that conclusion is likely to arouse the examiners' interest.

Are you enthusiastic about your subject?
Whatever the subject you choose, it's really important that you have some enthusiasm for it. Producing a dissertation is hard work, and you'll need some enthusiasm to sustain you when the going gets tough.

Ask the six questions in the above checklist about each of the possible subjects in your shortlist. Then compare your answers and make a choice. Ask your supervisor for help. He or she may well be able to point out aspects that haven't occurred to you. The fact that you have done your homework first will help to get you a sympathetic hearing.

When you have chosen your subject, write yourself a note with your answers to the checklist questions above. Pin this note up somewhere where you'll see it every time you sit down to work. Update it whenever you change something. You'll find it useful in keeping yourself on track, and particularly valuable when you come to write the introduction to your dissertation.

It's now time to start thinking about a title for your dissertation. Start to draw up a shortlist of alternative titles, especially if you are able or required to discuss your title with your supervisor. You will get a more useful reaction if you offer a selection than if you offer only one.

If you have to submit your title at an early stage and won't have the opportunity later to change it, make sure that you choose one that is not too restrictive, so it can accommodate changes in direction or emphasis that you may later find necessary. So something broad rather than narrow, general rather than precise, is needed. And don't make your title either a question or an answer.

Neat, informative and eye-catching titles often come in two parts, separated by a colon: a general statement, e.g. naming a field or a principle, followed by a particular one, indicating the precise area of your study. A title submitted at an early stage should not include this second part. You may be able to add it later, or add a subtitle, to give that extra detail.

What you should ask your teachers to do

When teachers are passing on to students the edict that they must submit a dissertation, it behoves them to give more thought to exactly what it is that they are asking students to do. The distinction between project and dissertation is a crucial one to make.

Chapter 11

Bored with reviewing the literature

Symptom

I've got to do a literature review for my dissertation. I've been working on it for ages, but there's so much to cover and now I've got really bogged down. I'm really bored with it and it's stopping me from getting on with my project.

Diagnosis

Welcome once again to a normal feature of academic life: academics requiring students to do things without teaching them how. Evidently your teachers haven't told or shown you what they expect a 'literature review' to contain, or how to produce – 'do' – one.

There is a deeper underlying issue here: How should you, as a student, use existing literature in carrying out and writing up a dissertation project?

I suggest that there are three distinct stages in using the literature. They involve 'relating' to the literature in three different ways:

(1) Exploring the literature: finding out what exists and is potentially useful to you, and perhaps classifying it, identifying the most important items and getting the general gist of them.

(2) Using the literature to create a 'platform' for your project: drawing out of it questions to answer, concepts to use, theories to test, controversies to resolve, debates to contribute to, and material for the discussion and conclusions chapters of your dissertation.

(3) Commenting on and criticizing the literature, having carried out your project, incorporating in your dissertation a critical discussion of significant items in the literature.

Clearly, to require you to do a 'literature review' without specifying which of the above is wanted will confuse you pretty thoroughly. I have seen many students who have interpreted this instruction as requiring them to do all three of the above, including commenting on and criticizing the literature before tackling their project, which is manifestly a nonsense and guaranteed to cause you stress: it's only when you are well advanced that you will be able to be properly critical of the books and articles that you are using.

Remedy

What you should do

Your first need is to make your own interpretation of 'literature review'. I suggest that you take it as the output from stage 2 above. That is to say, a literature review provides a platform for your project and material for discussion in your dissertation.

You clearly have to get stage 1 under your belt, then go on to stage 2.

(1) Exploring the literature

By 'the literature' I mean academic publications: books, articles, and theses or dissertations by academics or other scholars. To track down potentially useful academic publications:

- Make the most of any relevant reading lists that you have been given for your taught courses. Starting with the most recent publications listed, check out their references and bibliographies for leads to other books and articles.

- Make full use of your institution's library. Take advantage of any courses it runs in how to find useful publications, and consult the enquiry or help desk when you need assistance in finding your way around. If you haven't already done so, learn to use its computerized catalogue, and find out whether its computer system allows you to search for publications on your particular subject.

- Find out what specialist libraries there are in your field – many professional institutes and institutions maintain libraries at their headquarters – and investigate the possibility of gaining access to them. A student card and/or a letter from your head of department or supervisor may be needed for them to let you in. They may well have journals that your institution's library doesn't have.

- Identify the most relevant journals in your field and browse through recent numbers, checking out not only articles but also book reviews and letters to the editor for mentions of your subject.

- If there are prominent writers on your subject, look them up on a search engine, such as Google or Google Scholar. You might find a reference to a recent paper, or a recent or forthcoming lecture or conference appearance that's worth following up.

There are no short cuts. Don't expect anyone else to do this work for you. Once you've done some scouting around – but not before – consult your supervisor to see if there's anything that you've missed. You are much more likely to get useful help if you have already shown some initiative. The same applies if you want to consult experts elsewhere. A letter or an email along the lines 'I am making a study of ... What should I read?' is likely to go straight into the waste paper basket (trash).

As you explore the literature, start compiling your bibliography and collecting publications. A dissertation's bibliography is a list of the publications consulted by the writer. Every dissertation must have one. Start compiling yours straight away. Every time you come across a potentially useful publication, add it to your list. Be sure to record the essential details of all publications: author's names; titles of books and journals; titles of chapters in edited compilation books and articles in journals; publisher and year of publication; page numbers; etc. For an item on a web page you will need to record the URL (uniform resource locator) of the page, otherwise known as its web address, and the date on which you accessed the page.

When exploring the literature, all you want to know is whether a publication that you come across might be useful to you. When you find something that you think is potentially useful, write a little note to yourself about it, giving the details of the publication and your thoughts on how you might make use of it.

And when you're exploring the literature, try to hold off from starting to write your literature review. It's possible that your supervisor will ask you to show him or her a literature review early on, but try to get out of this, for three reasons. First, you don't know, when you're starting work, which pieces of literature will be relevant to your future work and which ones will not. Second, you are quite likely to uncover fresh sources as your work proceeds: it is not a good use of your time to redo work each time that you find a new source. Third, it may be that what your supervisor means by a 'literature review' is a summary of everything that has been written on the subject. Sadly, many students do attempt this. They collect a mass of books and photocopied articles, then sit down to write a potted summary of it all. Faced with this mass of publications, their task turns into a nightmare. They don't know where to start, they don't know how to organize their material, and when they start writing they soon find that they are in danger of their review taking up far too much of their time and far too many of the words at their disposal. Their 'literature review' turns into a premature review of the whole subject, and becomes a long essay in its own right. An absolute disaster.

(2) Creating your literature review

Remember that the purpose of your literature review is to create a 'platform' for your project. Such a platform can comprise one or more of the following:

- Questions – perhaps some questions posed in the literature, or questions that the literature has sparked off in your mind. Armed with these questions, you can then go on in your project to look for answers.

- Descriptions of phenomena, especially in case-study form. You could use these if you want to carry out a comparative study.

- A summary of the current debate on a topic. Here you could highlight differences between writers, and unresolved questions, and then go on in your project to explore these.

- An overview of the concepts and theories put forward by different writers. You could highlight similarities and differences, and then go on to test each one in terms of its internal consistency and its consistency with observations that you make.

- A summary of a particular writer's argument, which you then go on to test or to subject to a critique.

- An overview of an issue, where you highlight different perceptions of the issue and different proposals as to what actions should be taken, before developing your own proposals.

- A list of different aspects of a theme: you can then go on to discuss, taking each aspect in turn, what there is in the literature on each, before offering your own contribution.

- A review of different methodologies, highlighting the salient features of each, before going on to apply one or more.

- Literature can also provide background to a study: a historical background, for example. Such literature, because it is background rather than central, merits only a brief summary in your literature review.

Four final points about your literature review:

(1) Your coverage of the literature should be as comprehensive as you can make it. Don't run the risk of examiners saying that you have omitted to read something significant. If preparing a comprehensive literature review would require you to read hundreds of items, then almost certainly your subject is too broad – you must narrow it down – and has been 'done to death' by writers before you, leaving little or no scope for you to say anything interesting about it.

(2) Some sources are more academically impressive than others when cited in a dissertation. So don't reproduce chunks of text from standard textbooks or material by anonymous authors that you find on websites such as wikipedia. Depending on the subject and your teachers' predilections, references to material appearing in up-market newspapers might be acceptable, more particularly factual records of recent events and the utterances of participants in them, and comment by reputable academics rather than columnists.

(3) It is crucially important that you cite all your sources, i.e. give references for them, so that a reader can look them up for himself or herself if they wish. You must be meticulous about recording details of every verbatim quotation (indented or in quotation marks) that you include, of every piece of writing that you have paraphrased, and of writings, lectures, etc., the content of which you have digested and drawn on.

(4) Don't forget that when you have completed your project you will be in a far better position to deliver a critical appraisal of the literature than when you are writing your literature review. So save this for when you have completed your project and are writing it up.

What you should ask your teachers to do

Your teachers owe it to you to make it clear what they mean by 'literature review' and to give you some guidance in how to create one. They should abstain from making the unreasonable demand that you write a potted, critical summary of the literature before you have carried out your project.

Chapter 12

Feeling your opinion is worthless

Symptom

I've been told off for putting my own opinions and ideas into my essays. Isn't that what I'm supposed to do? I get the feeling my opinion is worthless.

Diagnosis

I have indeed had reports from some students that their teachers have said to them, on handing back an essay: 'I'm interested in what you've read, not in what you think.' If this has happened to you there's no need to be hurt or offended by it: you're getting useful feedback, even though it is discouraging.

But every such comment has to be put into context. There

could be more than one reason why the teacher who made that comment to you did so:

- If the comment was made early in the course, when it was necessary to get basic information under your belt before venturing into forming and presenting your own opinions and ideas, it could have been that your teacher felt you hadn't done that.

- When you include an opinion in an essay, you are exercising your judgment, and it has to be a mature, informed judgment exercised in the light of judgments that other people, especially authorities in the field, have made. In effect, you are joining in a debate, and you can't simply ignore the contributions that other people have made: perhaps that is what you did.

- Opinions need to be formed on the basis of knowledge and understanding: facts, analysis, etc. So you need to consider these in your essay before proceeding to state your opinion. It may have been that you stated your opinion without doing that, giving the unfortunate impression that you were just 'sounding off': academics won't be impressed by that.

- Ideas are best put forward tentatively, as hypotheses for testing rather than as firm conclusions. If you don't do this, if you don't test your ideas, again your teacher may be less than impressed.

Remedy

What you should do
My suggested remedies mostly follow from the above diagnosis:

- Get basic information under your belt before venturing into forming and presenting your own opinions and ideas.

- When you are writing a 'discuss-type' essay, think of what you are doing as contributing to a debate, and take account of the contributions that writers in the field have made before stating your opinion.

- Bear in mind that for an academic essay it is important that you form your opinions on the basis of knowledge and understanding: facts, analysis, etc. So consider these in your essay before proceeding to state your opinion.

- When putting ideas forward, do so tentatively, as hypotheses for testing rather than as firm conclusions. Consider how your ideas can be tested, and deal with that in your essay. Your teacher should be impressed by the thought you have put in.

What you should ask your teachers to do

Any teacher who utters to a student the disparaging comment 'I'm not interested in what you think' should be sent away for re-education, and not allowed to return to teaching until he or she has given thought to what it feels like to be on the receiving end of such a message.

Ask your teacher to demonstrate to you how to form opinions and place them within an essay, and to demonstrate the place of ideas in essays. In doing so, they should emphasize that every essay is the manifestation of a process of thinking, of reasoning, and demonstrate the part that ideas and opinions can and should play in those thinking and reasoning processes.

Chapter 13

Spooked by the plagiarism police

Symptom

We've had such strong warnings not to plagiarize that I don't trust myself to write anything.

Diagnosis

You aren't alone. Here's a snippet from *Online Scene*, published by the Southampton University Students' Union:

Plagiarism! Every student attempting to write an essay has the word ringing in their ears. It provokes the same fear in everyone whether you're a first year or you're writing your dissertation.[5]

The current concern with 'plagiarism' started out a few years ago as a concern among some academics that students were submitting written work that in whole or in part was composed by other people, without citing its source. In other words, they were passing off other people's writing as their own. In some cases this was clearly cheating – acting with intention to deceive. And it was particularly evident when large amounts of material had been 'lifted' – taken verbatim – from an unacknowledged source, or systematic efforts had been made to conceal the fact that other people's material has been used (e.g. by attributing only some of the 'borrowed' material, or changing the order of items in a list, or making minor alterations in wording).

Understandably, such cheating was taken particularly seriously when the mark for the work submitted counted towards the student's degree result. If not detected it could gain the perpetrator a better result than he or she had earned, potentially detrimental to the public standing of the institution's degrees, and grossly unfair to all the conscientious, law-abiding students who had worked hard for their results.

Universities have reacted to this situation by publishing regulations on plagiarism and issuing stern warnings, often couched in highly emotive language. New students may have to sign plagiarism statements immediately on arrival saying that they're aware of the seriousness of plagiarism and the penalties it incurs. So you turn up at uni, stand in a queue to register, are told 'sign here', and given no time to read the small print. The effect is to create a threatening, intimidating atmosphere, such as you appear to be experiencing.

We have also seen the growth of a corps of academic officers devoted to deterring and detecting plagiarism, and dealing with offenders – a kind of 'plagiarism police'. They are not the brightest stars in the academic firmament. They tend to use emotive language – plagiarism is 'cheating', 'dishonest', 'theft', 'stealing', 'a crime' – and often to use it incorrectly: 'theft', 'stealing' and 'crime' are terms with precise legal definitions, and plagiarism does not fall within any of them.[6] Many of their contributions to the literature on the subject reveal them to be unable to use extracts from other people's writings appropriately: thus we find factual statements prefaced by 'X argues' or 'Y suggests' as if they were matters of dispute, and judgments prefaced by 'X states' as if they were incontrovertible facts.[7]

And like all bureaucrats the plagiarism police tend to look for opportunities to expand their empire: not content with uncovering the purloining of the written word, some are attempting to extend their definition of 'plagiarism' to include 'the stealing of ideas', although ideas – as opposed to work based on them – cannot be copyrighted.[8] I find this very sad. Good teachers *give* ideas to students: they share them, contribute them to the common treasury of ideas. They think aloud in the company of students and spark off ideas jointly with them. They certainly don't communicate only in copyrightable media! That the plagiarism police can argue that ideas should be treated as property illustrates a woeful lack on their part of genuine academic spirit.

The plagiarism police also demonstrate a very shallow understanding of the phenomenon that they are addressing. They consistently take it for granted that a student who plagiarizes does so as the outcome of a rational calculation. Thus we find references to students who take '[a] decision to plagiarise', to students 'choosing to carry out plagiarism', to perceptions of 'common reasons for cheating' and to 'reasons' for plagiarism.[9] What we don't find is any understanding of the state of mind of students who are being tested on what they haven't been taught, who have problems in understanding the question, who are unclear about the criteria on which they are graded, who feel that the key to success lies in complying with some mysterious tacit code that they can't access, and who experience writing as a source of fear.[10]

Lynn Errey cites an international postgraduate student:

> When I get nervous about writing up my thoughts in poor English even when I know the subject okay I can't think. So I use other people's words.[11]

Take the emotional dimension – the stress – into account, and plagiarism begins to resemble the action of a drowning man clutching at a straw: no more rational than that. The plagiarism police have got it wrong again. And in zealously setting out to deter, detect and deal with plagiarism, they are simply jacking up the stress levels of the great mass of hard-working students, and increasing the likelihood that some will engage in the very behaviour that they are trying to stamp out.

Remedy

What you should do

It follows from the above diagnosis that the first thing you have to do is to lower the stress levels that writing creates for you, and indeed the preceding chapters in this book should all help you to do this. Discover what's wanted from you and what the 'rules of the game' are, and you'll find that this will calm you down considerably.

Second, develop good referencing practice. When you make notes for yourself, always include details of your sources, and when you write, cite your sources fully. This will go a long way to keeping you out of trouble with the plagiarism police.

Third, read the regulations that apply to you. Read them not only to discover the do's and don'ts, and the sanctions that can be inflicted on transgressors: pay attention to the language they use. If they describe potential offences in great detail and if they use emotive language and warn you about using 'other people's ideas', that's a sign that the plagiarism police are around. Your student officers should be closely monitoring the institution's treatment of alleged plagiarism. If it transpires that punished offences all involve nothing more esoteric than obvious cheating (individuals passing off other people's work as their own) you can probably relax: it's an indication that common sense is prevailing.

But there will always be some grey areas. Most academics would regard it as nothing more than a lapse from good academic practice if you accidentally failed to cite a source, or failed to attribute a phrase or two dimly recollected from a lecture, or failed to attribute the original of some well-thought-out paraphrasing, or omitted quotation marks from a quotation where you have actually cited the source, or made an error of judgement as to what can be treated as common knowledge. Usually these academics will be able to exercise a moderating influence on the zealots. Zealotry is not a good advertisement for a university.

Fourth, take care when working with other students. You will probably find that you are warned not only against committing plagiarism but also against committing 'collusion', conspiring with one or more other students to improve your marks by working together. Of course, students have always worked together – these may be among your most memorable and valuable learning experiences – and today we have the bizarre situation in many UK universities that on the one hand they are actually encouraging students to develop their teamwork skills, yet on the other hand they are warning them against collusion!

I would certainly encourage you to work with other students: you will learn from them as well as from your teachers, and you will usually be able to express ideas and ask questions without feeling that you are being judged, which may not be the case in 'official' tutorials, classes and seminars. And you may find essays written by other students easier to learn from than texts written by academics, because they are written by people who are at a similar stage of the learning process to yourself. But do stop short of drafting essays or parts of essays together. The final selection of words *must* emerge from your own mind: it must be your own. Otherwise the sniffers-out of plagiarism will be on your tracks.

Fifth, and finally, don't be tempted, even if you are up against a deadline, to buy an essay from an outfit advertising on the internet and submit it as your own work. This really is asking for trouble. Doing this raises no subtle questions of what is meant by 'plagiarism': it is an absolutely clear-cut case of cheating. The use today of highly developed software to reveal similarities in text makes it almost certain that you will be found out. You will be severely penalized – possibly being refused a degree or expelled from the institution – and subjected to a great deal of public humiliation, involving being branded as dishonest and a cheat. So I definitely do not recommend this course of action.

I would just add that in my experience students who actively try to master the language of their subjects, who question what they read, who read more than one book on a topic and check out original sources, and who actively seek feedback from their teachers and discuss their subjects with other students, tend to be the ones who get good results. Try to be one of them, and passing off other people's work as your own is the last thing you'll need to do in order to get good marks.

What you should ask your teachers to do

The most useful thing that your teachers could do to take the fear out of writing and reduce the incidence of plagiarism is to demystify the process of learning how to write academic essays.

Look at it like this. When you first meet academic-speak in printed form it's difficult to do anything more than make notes, by selecting and copying out material that you hope is relevant. That's stage 1 of the learning process. After a while you start paraphrasing, putting material in your own words: now you're translating the academic-speak into language that makes sense to you. That's stage 2 of the process. And after doing this for a while you find yourself thinking and reasoning in the subject's language: now you're there, 'digesting' the material and really engaging with the subject. That's stage 3, the final stage, of the process.

In my experience almost all teachers in essay-based subjects expect you to leap directly to stage 3 and they judge your work on that basis, which is extremely harsh and completely uncalled for. Try to explain to them the process that you are going through, because if they put their minds to it they can help you a great deal. In stage 1 they can help you to learn to judge the relevance of material, and train you in the habit of accurately citing the source of every note you make (referencing). In stage 2 they can check that your paraphrasing is accurate and appropriate and that you are continuing to reference correctly. They can then help you on to stage 3, and make sure that you have 'got it'. In this final stage, it may be difficult to tell where someone else's thoughts end and yours begin, so referencing can be a bit tricky: they can help you gain the experience and confidence you need to reference correctly, and avoid not only plagiarism but laying yourself open to the suspicion of plagiarism.

Don't be afraid to ask for help. Writing academic essays and learning to identify sources and cite them accurately do not come naturally to anyone, and as a student you are entitled to get help from those who are appointed as your teachers.

Chapter 14

Getting good marks for coursework, poor marks in exams

Symptom

I got good marks for my coursework during the year, but the marks I got for my exams in the summer were poor. The same thing happened last year too. What really upsets me is that I can't find out why.

Diagnosis

It's the usual routine in UK universities for the details of exam marks not to be disclosed to candidates, so you won't even be told which questions you answered well and which ones not so well. Consequently we have here another case where your university experience can come to feel like a bit of a nightmare: in effect you're playing a game in which you don't know the rules of the scoring system. You clearly know your subject matter, or you wouldn't have got good marks for your coursework, so I understand your bafflement and frustration at not being able to do well in exams.

I have worked with a number of students in the same situation as you. What we have done is to conduct a 'post-mortem': they reconstruct the answers that they gave in the exam and together we check them out. What has emerged from this exercise is that they were being marked not only on their knowledge of the subject *but also on their ability to 'decipher' the question*, to work out from the wording what the examiners wanted. I strongly suspect that the same was happening for you. And if you don't work out what the examiners want, you are bound to fare badly in your quest for marks. Do you recollect your teachers stressing to you in the run-up to exams: 'You *must* answer the question'? If you do, this is certainly what they were alluding to. But, characteristically, they weren't spelling out in language anyone could understand what they meant by 'answer the question': they weren't demonstrating to you *how* to do it.

Remedy

What you should do

When you read an exam question that is new to you almost certainly the first thing you will do is to register the area of knowledge that it covers. But you mustn't stop there. I repeat, you have to decipher the question, to 'read between the lines', to work out what it is that the examiners want. This often involves *challenging* the question, and you must never be afraid to do this.

If you have read and acted on Chapters 6 and 7 of this book, you have already mastered the basics of this art, because it is closely allied to interpretation of essay topics. The advice below, which has all been tried and tested, follows the paragraphs that make up the section on interpretation in Chapter 6.

(1) If the question uses terms that different writers use to mean different things, the examiners are 'fishing' to know whether you are aware of these different usages. So show them that you are. Don't just plump for the one usage that you prefer: outline at least two, and if you're choosing to answer on the basis of just one of them, say why you are choosing that one.

(2) If the question uses abstract and technical terms, it may be that the

examiners want you to demonstrate your understanding of these. If you think they do, then give definitions or translations into ordinary language, or use examples or illustrations for the purpose.

(3) If the question uses colloquial language and metaphors, it will be imprecise and 'woolly'. You may well be tempted to answer in the same imprecise and woolly language: don't! If you do, you are falling into a trap that the examiners have set for you. Answering in woolly and imprecise language will give them the impression that your thinking is woolly and imprecise, and indeed you will be hard-pressed to apply anything like a rigorous methodology (see Chapters 6 and 7 again). So translate colloquial language and metaphors into language that is appropriate to your discipline.

(4) If the question contains one or more generalizations, be aware that each generalization is presenting you with a trap: it is inviting you to respond to the question in equally general terms, and you will lose marks if you do that. So always challenge such generalizations. To use my earlier example, if you are asked why Latin America defaulted on its debts in the 1930s, you absolutely *must* distinguish in your answer between the different countries (or some of them) that comprise Latin America. If you fail to do this, and your answer merely refers to Latin America and not to any individual countries, there is no way that you can get a better than mediocre mark.

(5) If the question contains words that include or exclude or quantify, pay close attention to these: if you ignore them you are almost certainly falling into a trap. To avoid the trap, challenge even little words like 'all' or 'only'. To get good marks your essay may need to show that the statement, say, is true not of 'all' but of 'some', or not true of X 'only' but of 'others' such as Y and Z as well.

(6) Some questions may contain time-related words and expressions. These may specify dates, time spans, frequencies, etc: 'has/have been', 'has/have/will become', 'today', 'currently', 'still', 'rarely', 'sometimes', 'frequently', 'often', 'always'. Or they may specify time-related processes, such as 'development', 'evolution' and sequences and successions of events or situations. If you encounter these, it is crucial that you pay attention to these words and expressions and make it clear that you have done so. For example, 'today' and 'currently' require you to deal with the

present situation (or whatever) and you should definitely *not* write a historical answer. 'Still', however, does require a comparison between the present and the past. 'Development' and 'evolution' presume a relatively smooth process rather than one marked by sharp discontinuities, and you *must* show that you are aware of this.

(7) Some questions will incorporate wording that conveys a claim, assertion, judgement, opinion or an assumption of some kind. If you detect these (they may be hidden or not obvious), you should bring them out – make them explicit – and always test or challenge them. Do this by identifying any underlying 'biases' that they may have: e.g. a political point of view, a sociological theory, a value judgement, a partial selection of facts, or a skewed interpretation of facts.

(8) If the question contains wording that denotes cause and effect, like 'was significant', 'was responsible for', 'could not have taken place without', spell out the relationship that is being put forward. Then you must go on to consider (a) other possible causal factors in addition to the one suggested; (b) the mechanism or process linking cause(s) and effect; and (c) conditions or circumstances that can affect or could have affected the effect. (Remember that relevant factors can operate in a variety of ways: they can promote, motivate, facilitate, hinder, constitute resources or opportunities, etc.) You may also want to consider (d) 'counterfactuals', alternative (imagined) effects that might have come about but did not.

(9) You may well encounter questions with wording that – usually misleadingly – conveys degree or distance, such as 'How far ...?' and 'To what extent ...?' You must think about your methodology before starting to write. So ask yourself: 'How can I tell how far ...?' and: 'How can I tell to what extent ...?' If you're asked in a cause-and-effect question 'How far/to what extent was X responsible for ...?' you should interpret this as a question about X *in relation to other factors*, so your answer must deal with these other factors as well as X.

What you should ask your teachers to do

In my opinion, it is a disgrace, and reflects great discredit on UK institutions of higher education, that students' exam results depend not only on their knowledge of the subject but on their ability to identify and succeed in the word games that examiners play when setting exam questions. Having been an examiner myself I appreciate the pressures that examiners are under to invent new questions each year, but much could be done to make questions more straightforward and eliminate game-playing.

Because individual examiners are perhaps too close to their material to do this unaided, there should be procedures in place for other people to vet draft exam papers for intelligibility and straightforwardness. These procedures need to exist not only as a matter of policy: they should be strictly enforced. While colleagues and external examiners may currently cast their eyes over draft papers, intelligibility and straightforwardness are not necessarily at the forefront of their minds when they do so.

Even with these measures in force, lapses may occur. These should be identified and learned from. I suggest, therefore, that you ask your department to set up an 'exam paper review system' on the following lines. Every year, before exam papers are set, each cohort of students should be shown the exam paper sat by their immediate predecessors and invited to comment in writing on how intelligible and straightforward they judge the questions in that paper to be. Examiners should have those comments before them when setting the new paper.

If your department doesn't invite you to do this, there is no reason why you and your fellow students shouldn't take the initiative and do it 'off your own bat'. Get together, produce a list of comments on past papers, and submit it. Don't be afraid of making fools of yourselves. If you all put your heads together and still can't fathom what a question is seeking, that is a reflection on the question, not on you.

Chapter 15

Terrified by the prospect of exams

Symptom

The prospect of exams terrifies me. I don't like looking at past exam papers, and put it off as long as possible. I'm afraid I'll have a panic attack as I did once before. And other students are always talking about what will or won't come up in the exam and discussing what topics they are selecting to revise, which winds me up.

Diagnosis

There's a lot going on here. If you are terrified by the prospect of exams, as you say, or fear that you'll have a panic attack, that suggests that you are in effect running a movie for yourself, a 'disaster movie'. Perhaps you're taking events from your past and projecting them into the future. Keep running that movie over and over and it will get into your 'programming': it becomes a self-fulfilling prophecy.

And ask yourself why it is that you get wound up by hearing other students talking about what will or won't come up in the exam and discussing what topics they are selecting to revise. (Have you noticed, by the way, that some people take pleasure in winding others up?) What is it that makes you susceptible? A common cause is lack of confidence in one's own judgment: if every new 'scare' sets you off in a different direction that could be so in your case.

Remedy

What you should do

First, bear in mind that – as we saw in Chapter 12 – there are two requirements for success in exams. One is that you know your subject, your material. The other is that you have acquired the skill of interpreting exam questions. With that knowledge and that skill, you will have a flying start.

Now let's deal with the past exam papers. If they induce feelings of terror in you, the best way to inoculate yourself against this is to get to know them really well. (There's no way that something you're very familiar with can terrify you!) So do some work on them. Start today! Get in as much practice as you can at interpreting questions. Do some bullet-point answers. Look for answers to the questions in your textbooks and lecture notes. Work with a friend, if you like. Treat this as an exercise in learning what the examiners – who will often be your teachers – are looking for and how they think about their subject. Just imagine: when the exam comes you could go into the exam room, look at the exam paper, and what do you see there in front of you? Old familiar friends! That's the state of mind to aim at, and if you practise – train yourself in – interpreting questions of the kind that usually come up (e.g. questions beginning 'To what extent ...' or ending in 'Discuss') you'll find it's perfectly feasible to get into that state of mind.

As for the panic attack, please recollect and dwell on past exams that you've taken when you *didn't* have a panic attack. Picture yourself sitting one of those exams where you did well, remember how good it felt to be in charge and writing purposefully, tell yourself what a good experience it was. 'Anchor' that experience by associating it with a physical gesture. Call the memory to mind and while enjoying it do something like pressing the forefinger and thumb of one of your hands together. Do this a few times, and then making the gesture will become an effective technique for recalling the experience, a technique you can use at any time.[12]

If you're going to run a movie, why not do yourself a favour and make it one that has a happy ending? If an athlete started a race with his or her mind focused on 'problems', it would not be conducive to winning. It's the same for you. So envisage success! Go and take a look if you can at the room that you'll be sitting the exam in. Then run a movie of yourself sitting in the exam room creating essay plans and contentedly covering the pages of your answer book. You could even 'step into' the movie and start writing! It will certainly make working for exams more pleasurable if there are some plea-surable feelings associated with it.

I appreciate that you may not find this easy at first. Perhaps you had it drummed into you as a child: 'Don't count your chickens before they're hatched.' Recognize that you were being actively taught not to envisage success. It's a completely counter-productive message, of course: there's no better incentive to taking good care of eggs than the prospect of getting a chicken from each one. So, instead, envisage yourself actively helping eggs to hatch and taking pleasure in the results!

It may be that you're having a bad day and a disaster scenario insists on coming into your mind. Here's a tip. Run the movie forwards – you don't need to dwell on all the gory detail – *and then run it backwards, very very quickly, in just a few seconds.* If it's in colour, do the same again but in shades of grey this time. If it has a soundtrack, repeat the process with the sound turned down, then again with it turned off. Or you could run the movie as a video on a portable TV: put the TV on the back of a truck and as the truck drives off watch it get smaller and smaller and smaller and smaller and listen to the sound get quieter and quieter and quieter and quieter, and wave it goodbye as it disappears round a corner taking picture and sound with it.

This technique can be used with all sorts of variations. If still pictures come into your mind of situations you'd rather not be in, use your imagin-ation to deal with them. See them reflected in a distorting mirror. If they're in colour, turn people's faces lime green or beetroot red, or put the whole pic-ture into black and white. Put the picture in a frame, and tilt the frame away from you or turn it upside down. Experiment until you find a way of hand-ling the images that takes away their power to make you feel threatened.

Finally, avoid getting wound up by other students. At exam time we are particularly vulnerable to this. If you find you're getting wound up by someone, avoid their company. It isn't good for you. Don't get hooked into spending time or – especially – having meals with them. (It's not good for your digestion.) Stay away! Hang out with people who don't have to score points off you to feel good themselves.

What you should ask your teachers to do

In my experience, teachers are usually not helpful sources of advice on coping with exams, and are best not consulted unless you have a personal recommendation from another student or former student.

Chapter 16

In a project group sabotaged by a 'free-rider'

Symptom

*I've been put in a group with other
students and given a project to do. One
member of the group isn't pulling his weight.
He doesn't say much in meetings, and when he
says he will do something doesn't produce the
goods. He seems to be taking advantage of the fact
that we will all get the same mark for our project, so
however little he does he will benefit from the work the
rest of us do. It's both unfair and highly irritating.*

Diagnosis

Let's have a bit of background here. You and other students have
been thoroughly socialized throughout your educational experience into the ethos of 'individual achievement'. Learning is

something that you essentially do as an individual, and your exam marks, certificates and degree are awarded to you personally. Nowadays, some universities and departments are supposedly promoting 'teamwork' as part of their 'employability agenda', and doing this by forming students into groups – sometimes optimistically labelled 'teams' – and assigning them projects to do. However, there appears to be a widespread absence of assistance to students to work creatively and effectively as members of teams, and to deal with the interpersonal issues that inevitably come up in project work.

'Free-riding' is the name given to the behaviour of team members who deliberately limit the work that they put in, in the knowledge that they will nevertheless benefit from the efforts of the other members. Note that word 'deliberately': the implication is that you can see into their minds and identify the thoughts and feelings behind their behaviour. But these can be very complex, and you need to be very, very cautious about interpreting the behaviour that you see. Here are some possibilities.

It could be that your team-mate feels under pressure to devote more time and effort to the project than he feels is appropriate, and is backing out of doing the work entailed. So even though he has no intention of taking advantage of the work of the rest of you, he may appear to be doing so.

Alternatively, it could be that when tasks were allocated, the noisier and more forceful members of the group were the first to bid for those that they preferred, so it ended up that the quietest, most diffident member found himself left with a task for which he felt very ill-equipped. Such a person in that situation might nevertheless have felt it his duty to take the task on and did so, while keeping his fingers crossed that he would be able to master it. If he subsequently floundered, he may have been reluctant to ask for help, and instead withdrew: not turning up to meetings, not replying to emails, etc. Almost certainly he is experiencing a great deal of discomfort and stress, but the rest of you may conclude that he is deliberately free-riding.

It is almost inevitable, too, that at some times in the progress of a project some people will be doing more work than others. For example, a couple of people – with more advanced technical skills, perhaps, or a shared idea for the product – might effectively take charge of the project, and the others begin to feel that they're being shut out. The 'taking over' may not come about deliberately; if you are one of the 'activists' you are perhaps being carried along by your own enthusiasm and putting in two or three times as many hours as the other members. But if you're not one of the activists, you are very likely to feel unvalued, or undervalued. Indeed, you may be unable to see how you can make a contribution in these circumstances. So your motivation drops, and you don't work as hard or enthusiastically as you could – and your team-mates think you're free-riding.

The fourth possibility, of course, is that your team-mate simply has never learned how to work co-operatively with other people, and has no idea of how to do it and not the slightest inclination to learn.

Remedy

What you should do

The first thing is to find out what's in the supposedly free-riding student's mind. Is one of the above four scenarios in play? Or another, different one? Perhaps just one of you could talk to him (rather than summoning him to a 'trial by his peers'). A quiet talk may uncover what is really going on for him. It may be that he feels he has by now cut himself off from the team and you may be able to reassure him that the door is still open for him to return.

After such an exploratory talk, if he wants to come back on board and you want him to, there will need to be a meeting of the whole team. Each of you should say how you see the situation and how you feel about it. Note that this meeting is not – I repeat, *not* – an occasion for accusing or blaming. Indeed, statements beginning 'You are' should be avoided. What you can and should say is: 'This is how I see the situation, and this is how I feel about it.' The only person who is an authority on your perceptions and feelings is you, and you must speak up for yourself: no one can speak for you. And by the same token, you can speak for no one else.

Once perceptions and feelings are out in the open, and the air is cleared, you can compare your perceptions of what's going on. Are some individual tasks turning out to involve much more work than originally envisaged? Are the activists indeed charging along fuelled by their own enthusiasm? Is it indeed unclear what role the others can be taking on now?

Then it's time to turn to the question: How shall we proceed from this point on? Do you need to do more to acknowledge members' contributions? Do you need to make a fresh assessment of what tasks need to be carried out, and/or revise the allocation of tasks to individuals or pairs? Can some team members join in with the 'fun' work? Could some take on more of the workload later? Maybe those who have been feeling excluded will recover their motivation and involvement if the pair of activists carry on as they have been but make a point of reporting regularly to the others and consulting them on any issues they are faced with.

If, despite your efforts, you have clear evidence that there is some free-riding going on – someone is deliberately taking advantage of the rest of you and your hard work – it is, in my view, perfectly appropriate to let your teachers know about the situation and ask their help in dealing with it.

Perhaps, however, you feel that the issue is one that you should deal with yourselves. I suggest that the important thing to deal with is not so much the behaviour of the free-rider but your own feelings. It would not be surprising if you feel very angry and frustrated by the uncertainty that is inevitable when, say, someone takes away his individual tasks and then goes quiet and fails to come back to the group with the work he has done, or keeps making excuses but promises to deliver 'soon'. In this situation you don't know whether to do the work yourselves or to trust the other member and hold the project in abeyance until he produces, while hoping that what is produced will indeed be what is needed. The problem may be not so much that one member is unreliable and unproductive – aggravating though that is – but that the conscientious members are crippled by their feelings of anger towards the free-rider and frustration resulting from their inability to influence events and from their dependence on the free-rider.

In such a situation, your first priority has to be to free yourself from your dependence on the free-rider. You could have a 'last-ditch' strategy: ask the free-rider if he is encountering difficulties that he hasn't made known to the other members of the team; explain to him your difficulty with the situation you find yourselves in; give him a deadline for producing the work and agree among yourselves how you will do the work if it is not forthcoming from him.

Above all, though, you need a contingency plan. Not a contingency plan for what you will do if the free-rider doesn't produce, but a contingency plan for what you will do if he *does*. Plan your work programme on the basis that he *won't* produce (make sure, though, that you tell him what you are doing and why), but be prepared to react flexibly if – to your amazement – he does come up with the goods.

Dealing with free-riders can actually be a worthwhile learning experience for you, if you can develop strategies to channel your anger and frustration into positive action.

What you should ask your teachers to do

In setting up group projects, teachers are laying students open to very challenging and potentially stressful circumstances. It behoves them to exercise some care for their students, rather than abandoning them to events. They should get some training in facilitating groups and always be on hand. Make it clear to your teachers that you do not expect to be abandoned by them while your project is under way.

Teachers should certainly give some thought to the possibility that some students might try to take a free ride – if yours haven't, prod them! – and they should maximize the incentive to work as a team by providing for a proportion of marks to come from a self-and peer-assessment. Students can be asked to evaluate their own contributions and those of other team members, in terms of their attendance at meetings; how well they interact with others (including making it easy for others to join in); their contribution to planning the project, leadership and management; and their contribution to producing the deliverables. The idea is to make each of you more aware of how you are regarded by other members of your group. (A marking system can be adopted that disregards inflation of one's own marks, a self-assessment being ignored if it is appreciably higher – or lower – on any criterion than the aggregate assessment of that student supplied by the others.)

Chapter 17

Hopeless at time management

Symptom

I'm hopeless at managing my time. I'm always staying up late to finish work, then I oversleep and miss lectures and classes the next day. I keep setting myself deadlines – and then I can't keep to them. And I feel guilty if I take a day off.

Diagnosis

Clearly there's a complex three-way relationship between you, your work and time. It's the same for most students. Time plays a central part in your academic life. You're in an academic cycle that repeats year after year. During term or semester you'll have a weekly timetable, the 'treadmill'. Superimposed on these patterns are exams and hand-in dates for essays, project reports and other coursework. This combination of cycles and 'deadlines' is not an easy one for anyone to handle, although its trickiness often goes unacknowledged. The unquantifiable nature of learning – there's always more to read or check or discover – doesn't help either. And once something goes amiss, there's almost always a domino effect. As your experience shows, to finish one task you have to put off another, so your difficulties accumulate, getting worse each time.

So what's going on for you? Here are some self-diagnosis questions:

- Do you suspect that you may be trying to do too much, being unrealistically overambitious perhaps?
- Do you have difficulty in getting started and so keep putting things off?
- Are your work methods inefficient? (For example, are you a compulsive note-taker and a reader of every line in a book?)
- Are you always aiming for perfection, spending a long time in the pursuit of it but never actually attaining it?
- Do you think that you're poor at planning and putting your plans into effect: flitting from task to task, perhaps, rather than identifying a priority and concentrating your effort on it?

Remedy

What you should do

(1) If you suspect you're trying to do too much:

Here and now, take a few minutes to make a list of the jobs you've currently got to do and the dates they have to be finished by. Then make an estimate (as realistic as possible) of how many hours you ought to put in on each of those jobs in the next seven days. Add those 'hours required' together.

Now calculate your 'hours available'. Do this by deducting from 168 (7 × 24) the hours you need for sleep, meals (preparing, collecting, eating), personal care, travel, and attending lectures and classes.

Do your 'hours available' exceed your 'hours needed'? If so, brilliant! Congratulations! Or do your 'hours needed' exceed your 'hours available'? If that's the case, it's crunch time: you have some deciding to do. Negotiate an extension of a deadline; give priority to tasks that will count towards your degree result; dash off something rough and ready if that task is low priority. Whatever else you do, *do not* ignore the situation and bury your head in the sand: that will simply create more and more problems for you as successive dominoes collapse.

(2) If you keep putting things off:

Name something that you are putting off right now, at this very moment. See if you can identify whatever it is that is blocking you, the 'roadblock'. Now see if you can identify the roadblock behind that roadblock.

I'm suggesting this because almost always, in my experience, the first reason that people give for not being able to get on with a piece of work is not the real reason. 'There's another book I need to look at before I can get on with this essay' is likely to be a 'front' for 'I don't understand the topic' or 'I can't see how to get started'. And it's the real, underlying roadblock that you have to address before you can move on. In this example, however, many more books that you read won't get you any further with the essay: you have to get help with understanding the topic (interpreting it, actually) first.

(3) If your work methods are inefficient:

Try to put a name to every symptom of inefficiency that you're aware of. For example:

- Compulsive, unnecessary note-taking
- Reading stuff I don't have to in case I miss something
- Trying to work but not really knowing what I'm doing
- Repeating things I did earlier but getting the same result
- Getting 'bogged down'
- Going round in circles
- Getting distracted easily
- Allowing other people to disturb me and drag me off for coffee.

What strikes me about this list (besides the worrying realization that I found it very quick and easy to draw up!) is that these behaviours tend to be driven or facilitated by negative emotions – especially fear – rather than rational calculation. What's needed, I think, is a 'strategic' approach to your work, an approach that will enable you to stand back and see at the time – rather than in retrospect – what's happening when you're getting bogged down or whatever, and to take corrective action.

What does a strategic approach entail? If you're writing an essay on a set question on a subject that you're not familiar with, so you don't really know what you're doing, just starting to write is almost certainly not the best way to go about your task. Think strategic: work on interpreting the question (to clarify what you're expected to do), make a note of key terms that you need to look up, jot down notes for your introduction, and rough out a tentative structure for the essay. This will give you a 'bird's-eye view' of the job in hand, and make it much easier to assemble the final essay.

If you're getting bogged down with a piece of work that just won't 'come right', perhaps your (unconscious) strategy thus far has been 'If at first you don't succeed, try, try again.' The strategic approach would involve finding an alternative strategy, such as 'If at first you don't succeed, try something different.'

And if you suffer unduly from distractions and disturbances, the strategic approach would not be to tackle each as it arises but to put defences in place. You can do this in a variety of ways: e.g., by finding a place to work that is physically removed from sources of distraction and temptation; or, if you can settle on a regular work routine, 'ring-fencing' your study time against interruption by telling all your family and friends that you have made it an inflexible rule that you are not available during those hours.

(4) If you're always aiming for perfection:

Perfectionism is a trait that is less easy to detect in oneself than you might think. While one of the commonly accepted indicators is a reluctance to hand work in – we tell ourselves and anyone who asks: 'There's more that I need to do on it' – it could be that we started too late and haven't finished, or that there are mysterious psychological factors at work. Some people find it difficult to 'let go' of a piece of work, and/or are inhibited by the fact that their work will be exposed to the critical and perhaps unsympathetic gaze of another person.

Even if these other factors aren't present, the true perfectionist has a hard time of it. Forever seeking after perfection is liable to be enormously time-consuming. And in some subjects, especially essay-based ones where there is no right answer to a question, perfection is impossible to attain. If the other factors *are* present, being a perfectionist as well can make life quite a misery.

But there are certainly things you can do to make life easier for yourself and at the same time reduce significantly the hours you spend on every piece of work you hand in for marking. The principle here is 'reframing', learning to see and experience your situation in a different way. For example, at present you may – deep down, perhaps – view handing in work that is to be marked as exposing yourself to criticism or even belittling. With a spot of reframing you could learn to regard handing in a piece of work as entering a lottery: the result you get is in any case going to be to some extent the luck of the draw. Or you could regard it as a way of eliciting feedback from your teachers: of discovering what they want from you, getting a clearer idea of what their expectations of you are, and what you could do to improve the standard of your work. Here it is you who will be doing the judging, passing judgment on the quality of the feedback you're receiving.

(5) If you think you're poor at planning:

In the context of 'time management', 'planning' means 'planning ahead' (rather than 'designing'). Planning ahead is not easy where learning is involved, because everything you do is in some sense new, so there's always an element of uncertainty involved. You rarely have an exactly similar past experience to refer to, and you never know what tomorrow will bring: some new insight or piece of information may come your way that sets you off on a different track or sends you back to revise what you have spent the past three weeks writing.

There are two important things to bear in mind about planning. First, for it to be effective it must be part of a system of management that also incorporates provision for monitoring whether work is on track to accomplish planned outcomes, and for taking corrective action if it is not. Second, planning is about reconciling demands with resources.

Here are some suggestions to help you develop your planning skills:

- When a task is assigned to you, get into the habit of estimating how long it will take (hours, days or weeks).

- Monitor how good you are at keeping to deadlines, whether set by others or yourself.

- When starting on a task, think of your work on it as being divisible into a succession of stages, and give yourself a deadline for completing each one.

- It's quite possible that your order of priorities will have to change on a daily basis, so consciously review your priorities for the next day every evening.

Finally, there is a very simple but invaluable device for planning your use of time, for matching demands with resources: it's just a weekly timetable for use in term-time. You may have received your official timetable from the authorities in the form of a list of times and places, but do – *do!* – turn it into a chart at the earliest opportunity. Make it colourful: use different colours for different events, i.e. events in each series of lectures and seminars (classes). Now think about time that you want to use before (for preparing) and after (for writing up) each event. Choose suitable time-slots for these activities, and mark them on your timetable too. Having done that, see what wide open spaces you have left, and think about using these creatively. For example, it could be that you have a very heavy Monday and Tuesday, a lighter Wednesday and Thursday, and no formal teaching at all on Friday: in such a case you might consider shifting your weekend forward by a day – i.e. give yourself a Friday–Saturday weekend – and use Sunday for working, especially for preparing for the Monday and Tuesday ahead.

Carry a copy of your timetable with you at all times and stick a copy up on the wall of your room where you can easily see it. After a short while it will become a regular part of your life, and help to give you a working rhythm that will stand you in good stead.

Complement your weekly timetable with a diary and a wall-calendar or 'planner' wall-chart on which you can mark the one-off deadlines and other single events in your life, as well as basics like the beginnings and ends of terms/semesters and the 'number' of each week (e.g. the first Monday of term has a '1', the second Monday a '2', etc.). This too will help you to get accustomed to your pattern and to prevent one-off events from unduly disturbing your weekly routine.

What you should ask your teachers to do

There's probably not a lot that your teachers can do to help you with time management, but if you find deadlines from different teachers are clashing horrendously, see if you can negotiate moves or extensions of deadlines. This is a perfectly reasonable thing to ask for.

Chapter 18

Tongue-tied in seminars

Symptom

I find it difficult to participate in seminars and the prospect of having to give a presentation fills me with dread.

Diagnosis

Participation in a seminar can be very difficult, even if you want to contribute and have done some preparation beforehand. If you find yourself among 20 very talkative people, it may be extremely difficult to get a word in and then the opportunity passes and you've missed it. And you might come fully prepared and then find that the discussion goes off in a direction that you hadn't anticipated and are not prepared for. Furthermore, if your teacher has the habit of 'pouncing', putting a student on the spot with a question, this can lead to some students spending the entire seminar in a state of tension. If you've had experiences like this, you may be regarding forthcoming seminars with a degree of anxiety.

Having to give a presentation can be even more nerve-racking. You know that you'll be under the spotlight: everyone's eyes will be on you. Addressing an audience is something that many people dread. Even experienced presenters feel nervous before giving a presentation.

A touch of nerves immediately before giving a presentation is by no means a bad thing. They generate adrenalin, which will give you a buzz and keep you 'on your toes', and your presentation will be all the better for it. But if your presentation is days or weeks away and you're already getting sinking feelings in your stomach and can't eat or get to sleep at night, your nerves aren't helping you.

Nerves can be aroused merely by worrying, by thinking about all the things that could go wrong. This is your head at work. You're consciously anticipating a disaster: in your mind you can see, hear and feel all the elements of a disaster coming together. But the process can bypass your head altogether. Nerves can 'hit' you without warning – in your mouth, your throat or the pit of your stomach. Perhaps some traumatic moment from your childhood, buried in your subconscious, has been resurrected: your first day at school, perhaps, or an occasion when you were humiliated by a teacher.

Remedy

What you should do to make your participation in seminars less stressful

Here are some suggestions for making participation in seminars less stressful for yourself:

- Observe your teacher
- Do your homework
- Find techniques for getting into the discussion.

Observe your teacher. Notice your teacher's style. The best ones are like sheepdogs: they know what direction they want the seminar to take and marshal you all along in that direction. Once you're familiar with this style, think about how you can make contributions that will help the process along. Some teachers, though, tend to turn the seminar into a lecture, or do little more than keep the conversation going. If you have one or more like this, think about how seminars could be made more rewarding. You and your fellow students might ask your teacher to use some time to set out an agenda for the discussion, or to identify the important questions, or to end by giving a summary that draws the various strands of the discussion together.

Do your homework. This is perhaps *the* secret of successful seminar participation. Don't feel you have to make yourself an expert on the subject. Get yourself a bit of background, so you have some idea of what's important. Check out past exam questions. Look in the reading material for concepts, categories, theories, etc. that writers have employed to 'make sense' of the subject. (See the advice in Chapter 2.) And look out for omissions, inconsistencies and differences of opinion. Treat these as puzzles and questions that you can bring to the seminar. Indeed, try to make a habit of bringing one or more questions to every seminar. They have a twofold value: they show your teacher that you have applied your mind to the subject, and they will often make a worthwhile contribution to the discussion.

Find techniques for getting into the discussion. The sooner you get into the discussion, the sooner any stress you might feel disperses. But getting into the discussion gets more and more difficult the longer you keep your mouth shut. So get into it as early as you can. If you sit as near to facing your teacher as you can, that will maximize your chance of catching his or her eye and being asked to speak. If you feel diffident about voicing an opinion, put it in the form of a question. If necessary, keep saying 'Can I ask . . .?' until you get the chance to ask it. Take a deep breath each time so you can speak loudly. Another way of getting noticed is that school-room standby: just put your hand up.

What you should do to make giving presentations less stressful

- Clarify what is expected of you
- Do your homework
- Outline a structure for your presentation

- Create a draft and check that it is audience-friendly
- Prepare a handout
- Rehearse
- Conquer your nerves
- During your presentation, use body language and eye contact to create rapport with your audience.

Clarify what is expected of you. The first step to conquering your nerves is to get clarification on what you're expected to provide and to make a start on providing it. You need a brief, which will comprise a topic, like an essay topic, together with some guidance as to the treatment that is expected from you. For example, does your teacher want you to use case studies, or provide a review of the literature, or take sides in a current debate?

If you haven't been given a clear brief, ask for one! If that doesn't work, put together a very rough outline for a presentation – bullet points or headings will do – and ask 'Will this do?' 'Have I left out anything I ought to put in?'

You also need to know how much time you are allowed for your presentation. Five minutes? Ten? Twenty? Thirty? Again, if you aren't told, you must *ask*! There are few things worse than being halfway through a presentation and getting signals from your teacher that it's time for you to wind up.

Do your homework. Do the required reading and any other preparation that is called for. Do it as soon as you can, to give yourself time to think about it and go over it in your mind.

Outline a structure for your presentation. This involves more thinking. You could set about it in the same way as you would for an essay, but bear in mind that giving a presentation is a much more personal act than handing in an essay: you are in front of an audience, exposed to view. Treat your presentation as you would an essay and it's very difficult to be authentic: you are likely to find yourself speaking in someone else's voice, and sounding like a textbook or an authority on the field, which you are not.

In *Perfect Presentations!* Graham Topping and I suggest that you treat your presentation as the telling of a story: your story, the story of how you approached the topic, how you researched it, how you made sense of it, and how you arrived at your conclusion. This not only avoids the 'authority trap', because you are speaking in your own voice (you are indeed an authority on your own personal 'voyage of discovery'): it also provides you with a structure in the form of the chronological thread that runs through your story.

Create a draft and check that it is audience-friendly. Think of your draft as your 'script' for your presentation. This is *not* so you have something to read out word-for-word to your audience – that's a thoroughly bad idea – but because when you have typed out your script you can redraft it to make it more 'conversational' and thus more 'audience-friendly'. There are some basic rules to follow:

- Keep your sentences simple. Break up long and/or complex sentences into short, straightforward ones.

- If you need to use words or expressions that not everyone in your audience will be familiar with, include their definitions in a handout. (See below. If they hear a word that sets them off thinking 'What does that mean?' they become distracted, and you have lost them.)

- Use less formal language. For example, rather than saying 'It was calculated that …', say 'I worked out that …'

- Use numbered lists and brief repetition wherever you can. 'There are three things to notice. First, … The second thing to notice is … The third thing to notice is …'

Once you have redrafted your script to make it more conversational, read it aloud again and as you do so imagine that you are talking to some of your friends. As you read it, highlight or underline the words, phrases or sentences that you are emphasizing. And insert marks to show where you are pausing.

Prepare a handout. A handout is the perfect vehicle for diagrams, tables, lists of references and a bibliography. A neat-looking handout will also demonstrate that you have approached your task in an organized, systematic way and given thought to what would be helpful to your audience.

Rehearse. To give a really good presentation you *must* rehearse it. Even experienced presenters rehearse carefully. Rehearsing will help you to give your presentation without having to think self-consciously about what you're doing while you're doing it. It helps you to 'internalize' it, so you don't have to ask yourself consciously what comes next: if you have rehearsed it properly it will come to your mind automatically, like the next line of a poem or song lyric that you know well.

Take every opportunity to rehearse, wherever you are. And you'll find it very helpful if you can get a friend or a sympathetic fellow student to join you when you're rehearsing. Just practising talking about the subject to someone else will fix your sequence of points in your mind. And if you are giving a presentation in a language other than your own mother tongue, a native speaker of the language is a very good person to have around.

Rehearsing will also help you to get your timing right. Even experienced presenters often try to cram in more material than they have time for and end up talking too fast – even gabbling – or leaving out important points. So rehearse your presentation in full, talking at presentation speed, as many times as are necessary for you to be sure that you are familiar with your material and that it fits your allotted time.

Conquer your nerves. In the run-up to your presentation there are three things you can do to bring your nerves under control: appreciate the work you've done, change your view of yourself, and visualize success.

To appreciate the work you've done, collect together all the material you've prepared. Look at the sheer quantity of what you have in front of you. It is your safety net: it will protect you from falling to earth with a bump. And compare what you know about your topic now with what you knew when you started out: this will remind you how far you've progressed and how much you now have 'under your belt'.

You may need to change your view of yourself if you're not used to being the centre of attention, as a presenter necessarily is. You may feel uncomfortable and self-conscious in the spotlight. Perhaps you see yourself as a modest, self-effacing, limelight-shunning sort of person; a dependable supporter of others rather than a pushy, attention-grabbing loudmouth.

The problem with labelling yourself in this way is that it becomes a self-fulfilling negative prophecy. The more you tell yourself that you are a 'happiest in the background' sort of person, the more you close your mind to strategies that would help you to be comfortable in the foreground.

So take a minute or two to think back to a situation where you have been with other people and have felt comfortable and relaxed with them, able to be yourself, joining in the conversation and being listened to when you do. Picture the scene in your mind's eye: the room, the furniture, the company, etc. Hear again the conversation: yourself and the others speaking.

Recapture your feelings: the warmth you felt, your pleasure, your enjoyment, the sense of being appreciated and valued. Smile to yourself as you see that scene again, hear those sounds again, feel those pleasurable feelings again. Make a habit of doing this, with other past situations too, and you'll find yourself switching from negative to positive self-labelling.

Visualizing success will also help you. Prophecies, like labels, are often self-fulfilling. If you anticipate problems, you will certainly have problems. You'll be on the look-out for them, you'll tune in to them, they'll jump out at you. As I said in Chapter 13, if an athlete started a race with his or her mind focused on 'problems', it would not be conducive to winning. It's the same for you. So, open your mind to the possibility that your presentation will be a great success. Then it'll be ways of achieving success that spring to your attention.

If you can, go and take a look at the room that you'll be presenting in. Then in your mind's eye run a movie of yourself standing in that room giving your presentation. See, hear and feel yourself talking confidently, telling the story of the work you've done. Your behaviour will live up to the image that you have of yourself. That's how it works!

During your presentation, use body language and eye contact to create rapport with your audience. If you stand in front of your audience with your arms folded or held stiffly by your sides, and direct your eyes alternately to your notes and the ceiling, people in your audience are likely to slump in their seats and not look at you. If, however, you are using your hands to emphasize the points you are making, and offering eye contact to your audience – even just an occasional glance will do – they are more likely to take on a more alert posture and respond to your eyes with their own. And you are more likely to feel you are among friends, and respond by giving a really good presentation.

And get in the habit of smiling! Look at your audience and smile at everyone who is smiling at you. Then look around and smile at everyone else. Do this at the beginning and take advantage of every smile directed towards you to respond. But don't worry if not everybody smiles. Some will be concentrating on writing down your every word and some may have a sensational hangover from the night before! Make allowances for them!

What you should ask your teachers to do

I suggested above (p. 84) some requests that, as seminar participants, you and your fellow students might make to your teacher to make seminars more rewarding and thus less stressful.

There are several things that teachers can and should do to encourage novice presenters. Ask them to provide briefs that make their expectations clear, if they don't already. They should set a warm and encouraging tone to proceedings. And they should give constructive feedback but refrain from making formal on-the-spot assessments. Try to discourage anyone who is in the habit of doing this. Point out that such assessments make novices nervous and serve no educational purpose whatever.

Chapter 19

Unsure about the quality of counselling

Symptom

I've had some personal problems, which were stopping me from concentrating on my work. And I was missing classes and avoiding my teachers. So I went to see a counsellor who works for the student counselling service here. The first time was helpful, but since then after my visits I often don't feel better: I feel worse. And I still can't get down to work.

Diagnosis

What's going on here? Counselling is supposed to help you to cope with your distress. The idea is that when you talk in confidence to a trained counsellor – someone who isn't a friend or family member, and who is trained to listen carefully to 'clients' –

you are able to explore your feelings and talk about your problems and find ways of dealing with them.[13] So why isn't this constructive outcome happening for you?

Talking to a counsellor should enable you to stand back – distance yourself – from your problems, and view them from a new and helpful perspective, as if they were someone else's. From this standpoint, and with the counsellor's help, you should be able to find a way or ways forward that you couldn't see if you were deeply immersed in your problems.

That's the theory. The practice, however, is not always so straightforward. Current problems almost always have some roots in past experiences, and I have come across a number of cases where the counsellor has focused more on exploring those past experiences and the distress they caused than in addressing current problems. The result is that the distress, or the memory of it, is kept alive for the client. You keep returning to your distress – you keep being reminded of the painful feelings that you experienced in the past – and instead of moving on you find that you are 'stuck' in your past emotions and patterns of behaviour.

If, after seeing your counsellor, you feel worse when you leave than when you went in, it seems all too likely that the session was indeed doing more to resurrect past distress than to find a way forward for you.

Remedy

What you should do
There are some good, practical things you can do.

Work can often be the best therapy. Find a piece of work, however small, that you can make a start on *now*: start it, get absorbed in it. A problem to solve, a puzzle of some kind, something to write a short note on: these can all be good things to take. Then move on to another bite-sized piece of work. Rediscover the *fun* of tackling problems, puzzles or writing short pieces. Regain the confidence that comes with finding that you are still able to concentrate on work.

If you are someone whose normal way of dealing with painful emotions is to repress them – to bottle them up – try acknowledging them instead. Next time some past, distressing experience comes to mind, say to yourself something along these lines: 'Yes, that happened. It was horrible. I

Table 1: Bad counsellor, good counsellor: some distinguishing features

Bad counsellor	Good counsellor
Tells you a lot about himself	Will introduce himself briefly, but thereafter says very little or nothing about himself
Makes it clear he's very proud of his qualifications	May mention his qualifications and experience very briefly when he introduces himself, if he thinks it will provide some assurance to you of his bona fides, but won't talk about them subsequently
Gets emotionally involved in the story you tell him	Knows that he is of no use to you if he gets emotionally involved in your story. Will empathize and sympathize with you, but won't experience your emotions with anything like the intensity that you experience them. Stays calm
Gives advice and gets upset if you don't take it	Makes a range of suggestions: you feel free to pick and choose among them without upsetting him
Urges you to take medication against your better judgement	Might suggest that you take medical advice, and if he has experience of the effect of medications on previous clients he might tell you about that
Treats your past distress as the main subject of your session	Treats finding a way forward as the main subject of your session, reflecting on the past only if it generates 'solutions'
Makes it clear that he thinks he knows you better than you know yourself	Acknowledges that the expert on you is – you
Something of the voyeur about him: seems to get a kind of satisfaction from seeing you wallowing in misery	You never get the feeling that you're under the microscope, as if you were a subject of research
Even if you're distressed sends you out into the street when your hour is up	Helps you to start getting yourself together well before the end of your session

acknowledge the pain and distress it caused me. But I can't rewrite history. At some point in the future, probably when I'm not being subjected to the stresses of a student's life, I may want to get it out of my system through psychotherapy or psychoanalysis. But right now what I'm looking for are immediate practical steps that will enable me to get on with my studies.'

This is also a message that you can give to your counsellor. It is all too easy, especially when you encounter a counsellor for the first time and don't know quite what to expect, to let him or her set the tone and agenda of your meetings. After all, they are the ones with experience and qualifications, it's their office or consulting room, and they have a place in the institution's power structure. But don't be intimidated. As the client, you should expect to *share* in setting the tone and agenda, and you can afford to be assertive about this. If the counsellor resists, you need to find another counsellor.

If you need or want to find another counsellor, you need some way of telling the good from the bad. The information in Table 19.1 should help:

What you should ask your teachers to do

Teachers often refer students to counsellors. Usually, they do so after listening to you carefully and concluding you need expert help, though some – at the other extreme – are unable to cope with any personal 'stuff' and are relieved to get you off their hands. It would not be appropriate for teachers to enquire what went on in a counselling session, but if you want to you can volunteer the information and say whether you found the session helpful. You can say as much or as little as you want, but your feedback will enable them to form some judgement about the quality of the counselling on offer, and this could help them when they consider referring other students to the service.

Chapter 20

Feeling like dropping out

Symptom

I feel I don't belong here. I'm doing a modular degree: my courses are provided by four different departments and I don't feel I belong in any of them. All in all, I feel terribly unsupported and very confused. I'm thinking of dropping out.

Diagnosis

These and similar words are characteristically uttered by people who are feeling alienated from the culture and ethos of their institution.

We have seen in previous chapters how, as a student, you have to suss out for yourself how your teachers think, and what the expectations of you are. You're addressed in a special language that you aren't directly taught. You're tested on what you haven't been taught, and the widespread attitude – encouraged by the bodies that oversee higher education – that education is a matter of 'delivery' of knowledge, skills, etc., fosters the 'take it or leave it' attitude among teachers that it is up to you what use you make of the material that is 'left on your doorstep'. You get the message that learning is what you are expected to supply for yourself in between receiving teaching and being examined, but no one tells you how to supply it. You experience university not as educating but as mystifying, as an institution in which you are playing games, the rules of which are hidden from you, so you don't know what you have to do to win. You are made well aware of your place in the scheme of things if your essays are returned late and with only cursory comments, if you are only allowed half-a-dozen contact hours with staff per week, if it's difficult to get hold of teachers, and if as an undergraduate you are taught not by full-time academics but by PhD students who have not been trained to teach.

And in these days of higher education as a mass business, with more reliance on e-learning and less on one-to-one contact between students and teachers (who in any case have to give priority to publishing their research if they value their careers), you might well feel you're being treated as just another item passing along a production line.

Matters can only be worse if you're taking a 'modular' or joint honours degree, one made up of courses from perhaps as many as four different departments. Which teachers will you be learning to think like? The answer is evident: you won't be learning to think like anyone in particular. The risk is that you won't be learning to think in any organized way at all, because while you are exposed to a variety of mindsets no one has the job of helping you to see how they fit together (or not). And you are liable to find yourself in a completely different student group for each of the subjects you are taking and not belonging to any particular department in the university. The consequent 'bittiness' of such programmes and the absence of a social infrastructure makes them far more demanding than programmes provided for specialists.

Anyone studying at a UK university is liable to feel alienated at some time or other, but students who have come straight from school, mature students, international students and UK students from working-class backgrounds are perhaps most susceptible to such feelings because there are other factors compounding the situation.

If you have come straight from school, you may find it difficult to adapt to a teaching regime where you are left to your own devices a lot, with large empty spaces in your timetable and much less oversight by your teachers. If you are a mature student, you may sometimes feel very unvalued. Out in the 'real world' you are respected and your views count for something, but in the academic world neither may be the case. If you are from a working-class background, and especially if you're the first in your family to attend university, you may simply find the elitism and mind games of the academic world very off-putting. And if you are an international student, you are quite likely to find yourself in a teaching and examining regime that is very different from the one you are accustomed to, with very different rules and expectations.

If you weren't familiar with the UK university culture, you might also have found yourself channelled into a modular degree programme. A study by Bekhradnia and Aston of the different retention rates at the University of North London and London Guildhall University (merged in 2002 into London Metropolitan University) found that at UNL, where the dropout rate among first-year students was much higher, there was a much greater range of combinations and options available to students. 'This may have had an impact on dropout', they say, cautiously.[14]

Remedy

What you should do

If you are feeling you don't belong on your degree programme, and you feel that you have to take a decision – to pull out or to continue – it's a decision for you alone: no one else can take it for you. But before you take it, here are some things I suggest you ought to consider, and some questions to put to yourself:

(1) Be aware of what's going on for you. Reread the above paragraphs in this chapter, and notice all the pressures acting on you to destabilize you, to reduce your self-confidence and cause you to doubt yourself. Take a look at yourself in the context of those pressures, and appreciate the resilience you have already shown in not being completely ground down by them. And remind yourself of the academic ability that you know you possess, the ability that got you to uni in the first place.

(2) Be aware too that, if you are able to stay, things are quite likely to get better in your second year. I have seen many students 'click', even after poor first-year results. The great majority do better in their second year than in their first.

(3) Ask yourself: If I were starting my degree again would I do anything differently, e.g. in using my time better or making better use of the resources available to me? If you would, you have gained some valuable experience, and you have some encouragement to hang on in there and make use of it.

(4) Ask yourself: What have I got from uni so far? Look back at where you were when you started: what changes can you detect in yourself? Ask friends whom you trust what changes in you they can detect. (I'd be amazed if you and they can't between you detect any changes!) If you recognize some positive changes, are they ones that could develop or be added to if you stayed on? And ask what you have learned? If the benefits have been worthwhile, does that lead you to think that it's worth staying on?

(5) Ask yourself too: What do I want from uni? A degree? Perhaps one that will lead on to a job – or, better still, a career or vocation? If you leave, might there be alternative ways of getting on to a career ladder: working and studying part time, for example? Or is the qualification dangled in front of you less important than the opportunity of learning about a subject, or making sense of experience you've had out in the 'real world'? If you can make your goals explicit, that could help you in taking a 'stay-or-leave' decision.

(6) You may already have asked yourself: If I leave, what would I be writing off, what would I be losing? Think very hard about whether, if you think that staying on is not on balance the best thing for you, the fact that you have already invested a year should keep you in place. Similarly, would you be staying on purely to avoid 'losing face', as you see it? Sometimes writing off is the best thing to do, if the alternative is 'to throw good money after bad'. Charge your loss to experience!

(7) Next question: If you leave, what doors – if any – would you like to keep open? If you can take and pass your first-year exams you'll almost certainly have the opportunity to resume your degree programme at a later

date. And, if you might want to return to higher education at a different university, you'll stand a better chance of being admitted. It's always worth looking ahead to future possibilities, even if they seem unlikely ones at the moment.

(8) Final question. Before you take a no-going-back decision, you owe it to yourself to ask what the alternatives are to leaving. Could you simply take a year out from studying? I've known students who have got a lot of benefit from doing this: they have come back with a renewed determination to succeed and a clearer view of what they have to do to succeed. Alternatively, would a change of programme do the trick for you? If you've been taking a modular programme and found yourself falling between four stools, but enjoying one of your subjects in particular, you may get a renewed impetus from being able to concentrate on that subject. It's a possibility worth investigating.

I'd like to end by saying this. It is easy to see withdrawal from a university course as failure, and that is the prevailing view among academics, of course. There are other ways of looking at it, however. You have ventured into the academic world, with its special languages, its worshipping of the written word, its ethos of individual achievement, and its tendency to lapse into mystifying rather than educating. But there is another world, the 'real' world, with practical people doing practical things with skill and flair, a world of ingenuity and problem-solving, a world where people work together and learn by experiment and experience. This too is a world worthy of your effort and worth striving in to make the most of your potential. Do not measure your self-esteem and self-respect by your ability to jump through the artificial hoops that academics set for you.

What you should ask your teachers to do

In recent years universities have been given financial incentives by the government to 'widen participation', i.e. to recruit more students from socio-economic groups that in the past have been under-represented in higher education. However, this stimulus has not been matched by financial or other kind of encouragement to widen 'retention', to take steps to hold on to the 'widened participants'. Consequently, in some institutions we find a 'successful' widening participation programme but a relatively high withdrawal rate among first-year students. More students have been taken on, but a higher proportion have left too.

So try to give your teachers some understanding of the experience that you as a student have had at university. It might prompt at least some to treat students with the respect due to them as junior members of the community that a university ought to be.

Queries, feedback, updates, web links

If you have any queries about conquering study stress that this book hasn't covered, or any suggestions for improving the book, please log on to my personal website at:

www.student-friendly-guides.com

and send me an email. I'll be glad to answer any queries, and all suggestions for improvements will be very gratefully received. And don't forget to check out the web site regularly for updates to this and other student-friendly guides, and for useful web links.

Peter Levin

Notes and references

1 The term 'negative feedback' is nowadays commonly used to mean 'unconstructive response', and that is how I am using it here. This meaning is almost the exact opposite to the original meaning in the science of control systems, where negative feedback is used to correct a deviation from a target and thus keep a process on track: it is thus extremely constructive.

2 Report of the National Committee of Inquiry into Higher Education (Chairman Sir Ron Dearing), *Higher Education in the Learning Society* (NCIHE 1997), Para. 8.17.

3 *The National Student Survey 2006*, Report to HEFCE by Paula Surridge, Higher Education Funding Council for England, July 2007. Available online at *http://www.hefce.ac.uk/pubs/rdreports/2007/rd14_07/rd14_07.pdf*, last accessed 19 August 2007. See page 20. Only 51 per cent of respondents agreed with the statement 'Feedback on my work has been prompt'; only 57 per cent agreed that 'I have received detailed comments on my work'; only 51 per cent agreed that 'Feedback on my work has helped me clarify things I did not understand'.

4 This technique is based on the NLP spelling strategy invented by Robert Dilts. See http://www.nlpu.com/Articles/artic10.htm, last accessed 14 May 2007, and note 12.

5 'Students cheating to the top', *Online Scene*, 29 December 2005. Available online at http://www.wessexscene.co.uk/print.php?sid=1393, last accessed 14 May 2007.

6 For documented examples, see Peter Levin, *Why the Writing is on the Wall for the Plagiarism Police*, 1 June 2006. Available online at http://www.student-friendly-guides.com/plagiarism/writing_on_the_wall.pdf, last accessed 14 May 2007. See pp. 13–14.

7 *Ibid.*, pp. 15–16.

8 *Ibid.*, p.14.

9 *Ibid.*, pp. 12–13.

10 *Ibid.*, pp. 3–12. These observations of the state of mind of students are taken from S. Davies, D. Swinburne and G. Williams (eds), *Writing Matters: The Royal Literary Fund Report on Student Writing in Higher Education*, p. 1. (Royal Literary Fund, March 2006.) Available online at www.rlf.org.uk/fellowshipscheme/documents/RLF writingmatters_000.pdf, last accessed 11 May 2007.

11 L. Errey, 'Plagiarism: Something fishy? ... Or just a fish out of water?' *Teaching Forum*, Vol. 50, p.18 (Autumn 2002). Available online at http://www.brookes.ac.uk/virtual/NewTF/50/T50errey.pdf, last accessed 14 May 2007.

12 This and the other exercises are taken from a field of endeavour known as neuro-linguistic programming. There are several introductory texts on this subject including: Steve Andreas and Charles Faulkner (eds), *NLP: The New Technology of Achievement* (Nicholas Brealey 1996).
Joseph O'Connor and John Seymour, *Introducing Neuro-Linguistic Programming* (2nd revised edition, HarperCollins 2003).
Romilla Ready and Kate Burton, *Neuro-Linguistic Programming for Dummies* (John Wiley & Sons 2004).

13 This definition is taken from the 'Counselling Directory' website at: http://www.counselling-directory.org.uk/counselling.html, last accessed 14 May 2007.

14 Bahram Bekhradnia and Libby Aston, *Non-completion at the University of North London and London Guildhall University: a case study*, Higher Education Policy Institute, January 2005. Available online at http://www.hepi.ac.uk/pub-detail.asp?ID=168&DOC=Reports last accessed 14 May 2007.

Successful teamwork!

Peter Levin

This short, practical guide is for students who find themselves placed in groups and assigned a project to carry out.

* Allocating work appropriately
* Dealing with people who are taking a 'free-ride'
* Resolving disagreements
* Working constructively with people who they don't like very much.

The guide helps students to appreciate the tensions between the demands of the task, the needs of the team and individual's needs, and to understand why people behave as they do in a team situation. It provides reassurance when things get stressful, and helps students learn from the experience and make a success of their project.

Contents: Part One: Basics and Context – What do we mean by 'a team'? – The benefits of working in a team – Teamwork skills – Academic teamwork and the job market – Part Two: Getting Started – Get in your groups – Get to know one another – Formulate your ground rules – Check out your assignment and plan your work – Part Three: How are we Doing? – Progress on the project – Progress from 'group' to 'team' – Personal progress – Part Four: Perspectives on Team Behaviour – Tensions: the task, the team and the individual – Team roles – Management systems and team organization – Team development: forming, storming, norming, performing ... – The decision-making process – Negotiation – Cultural traits and differences – Individual traits: 'cats' and 'dogs' – Part Five: Teamwork Issues and Solutions – The task: getting the work done – Personal and inter-personal issues – Part Six: Benefiting from the Experience – Getting feedback – Reflection – Applying for jobs

136pp   0 335 21578 5 (Paperback)

Student Friendly Guides

Write great essays!

Peter Levin

What every student needs for university reading and writing!

- How can students find what they need from the long lists of recommended reading?
- What kind of notes should they take?
- What is the best way to structure an essay?
- How can plagiarism be avoided?

This lively, short, and to-the-point guide helps students to study and write effectively. Practical hints and suggestions which really work are coupled with insights into academic writing, critical reading and methods of presentation.

This guide builds confidence and changes study habits so students can get the grades they really deserve for the work they put in. No student should be without it!

136pp   0 335 21577 7   (Paperback)

GradeGuru

notes sharing by students for studer

So......now you are a

STAR STUDENT

and have conquered your

coursework. Did you

know that you can get **REWARDS** an

further recognition for the work

you have done? Get lots of

cool stuff and help your peer

by sharing your study notes online

To participate, or just to find ou

more, go to

www.gradeguru.com